The Great Agnostic

Robert Green Ingersoll, 1877

The Great Agnostic

Robert Ingersoll and
American Freethought

Susan Jacoby

Yale UNIVERSITY PRESS
NEW HAVEN & LONDON

Yale University Press books may be purchased in quantity for educational, business, or promotional use. For information, please e-mail
sales.press@yale.edu (U.S. office) or sales@yaleup.co.uk (U.K. office).

Set in Janson type by Integrated Publishing Solutions.
Printed in the United States of America.

Library of Congress Cataloging-in-Publication Data

Jacoby, Susan, 1945–
The great agnostic : Robert Ingersoll and American freethought /
Susan Jacoby.
    p. cm.
Includes bibliographical references (p.) and index.
ISBN 978-0-300-13725-5 (clothbound : alk. paper)

1. Ingersoll, Robert Green, 1833–1899. 2. Freethinkers—United
States—Biography. 3. Freethinkers—United States—History.
I. Title.
BL2790.I6J33   2013
211′.7092—dc23   2012027881

A catalogue record for this book is available from the British Library.

This paper meets the requirements of
ANSI/NISO Z39.48-1992 (Permanence of Paper).

10 9 8 7 6 5 4 3 2 1

In memory of Aaron Asher

The most formidable weapon against errors of every kind is reason.
—THOMAS PAINE

Contents

Contents

Acknowledgments

I wish to thank my editor at Yale, Christopher Rogers, for taking on this project; James Johnson for designing the perfect, evocative cover; Joyce Ippolito for an outstanding job of copy editing, including her identification of several words I have been misspelling since childhood; and Laura Jones Dooley for her second look.

As always, I am grateful for the efforts of my longtime literary agents, Georges and Anne Borchardt.

Finally, I wish to thank Jay Barksdale and to say that this book was written in the Allen Room under the shadow of the lions at that great institution, the New York Public Library.

Introduction

How and why do some public figures who were famous in their own time become part of a nation's historical memory, while others fade away or are confined to what is known on the Internet as "niche fame"? Robert Green Ingersoll (1833–1899), known in the last quarter of the nineteenth century as the "Great Agnostic," once possessed real fame as one of the two most important champions of reason and secular government in American history—the other being Thomas Paine. Indeed, one of Ingersoll's lasting accomplishments as the preeminent American orator of his era was the revival of Paine in the historical imagination of a nation that had been the beneficiary, throughout its revolutionary era, of some of the most memorable words ever written in the cause of liberty.

Ingersoll stepped onto the public stage as the leading figure in what historians of American secularism consider the golden age of freethought—an era when immigration, industrialization, and science, especially Charles Darwin's theory of evolution by means of natural selection, were challenging both religious orthodoxy and the supposedly simpler values of the nation's rural Anglo-Saxon past. That things were never really so simple was the message Ingersoll repeatedly conveyed as he spoke before more of his countrymen than elected public leaders, including presidents, in an era when lectures were both a form of mass entertainment and a vital source of information. Traveling across the continent at a time when most Americans did not, he spread his message not only to urban audiences but to those who had ridden miles on horseback to hear him speak in towns set down on the prairies of the Middle West and the cattle-grazing lands of the Southwest. Between 1875 and his death in 1899, Ingersoll spoke in every state except Mississippi, North Carolina, and Oklahoma. Known as "Robert Injuresoul" to his clerical enemies, he raised the issue of what role religion ought to play in the public life of the American nation for the first time since the writing of the Constitution, when the founders deliberately left out any acknowledgment of a deity as the source of governmental power. Ingersoll said of the founders:

They knew that to put God in the Constitution was to put man out. They knew that the recognition of a Deity would be seized upon by fanatics and zealots as a pretext for destroying the liberty of thought. They knew the terrible history of the church too well to place in her keeping, or in the keeping of her God, the sacred rights of man. They intended that all should have the right to worship, or not to worship; that our laws should make no distinction on account of creed. They intended to found and frame a government for man, and for man alone. They wished to preserve the individuality of all; to prevent the few from governing the many, and the many from persecuting and destroying the few.[1]

Of course, this view of the founders' intentions is far from universally accepted in the United States today. It is unlikely that any American politician with national ambitions would dare describe the secular spirit and letter of the Constitution so forthrightly in the twenty-first century. *They knew that to put God in the Constitution was to put man out.* It is all too easy to envision this sentence in a thirty-second attack ad on a modern politician who openly advocates secular values, yet the undeniable absence of God from the Constitution poses a serious historical problem for pious "originalists" who, while insisting that the

Constitution can mean only what its precise wording laid out in the eighteenth century, are equally insistent that the framers intended to establish a Christian government. I am certain that Ingersoll, given the faith of nineteenth-century freethinkers in the ultimate demise of rigid biblical religion, could never have imagined an America in which, more than a century after his death, a candidate for a major party's presidential nomination would declare that the very idea of absolute separation of church and state was enough "to make you throw up."* Ingersoll would have been even more astonished, given his generation's faith in education and technology, at the same candidate's dismissal of universal higher education as something that only a snob would support.

To the question that retains its politically divisive power today—whether the United States was founded as a Christian nation—Ingersoll answered an emphatic no. The marvel of the framers, he argued, was that they established "the first secular government that was ever

---

* This remark was made by former Pennsylvania Senator Rick Santorum, a devout and devoutly conservative Catholic, on a Sunday morning television news show in February 2012. He was, ironically, disparaging John F. Kennedy, the nation's first Catholic president, for having famously told a group of Protestant ministers during his 1960 campaign that he believed "in an America where the separation of church and state is absolute—where no church or church school is granted any public funds or political preference." Earlier in the week, after President Barack Obama had suggested that every American ought to be able to go to college, Santorum's reaction was, "What a snob!"

founded in this world" at a time when every government in Europe was still based on union between church and state.[2] "Recollect that," Ingersoll admonished his audience in a centennial oration, delivered on July 4, 1876, in his home town of Peoria, Illinois. "The first secular government; the first government that said every church has exactly the same rights and no more; every religion has the same rights, and no more. In other words, our fathers were the first men who had the sense, had the genius, to know that no church should be allowed to have a sword."[3] A government that had "retired the gods from politics," Ingersoll declared with decidedly premature optimism on America's hundredth birthday, was an indispensable condition of progress.[4] To nineteenth-century freethinkers, as to their eighteenth-century predecessors, intellectual and material progress went hand-in-hand with abandonment of superstition, and strong ties between government and religion amounted to state-endorsed superstition. Born decades before cities were illuminated by electricity, before the role of bacteria in the transmission of disease was understood, before Darwin's revolutionary insight that humans were descended from lower animals was fully accepted even within the scientific community, Ingersoll was the most outspoken and influential voice in a movement that was to forge a secular intellectual bridge into the twentieth century for many of his countrymen.

From a twenty-first-century perspective, it is clear that the golden age of freethought, which stretched roughly from 1875 until the beginning of the First World War, divided Americans in much the same fashion, and over many of the same issues, as the culture wars of the past three decades. Even though the religious, ethnic, and economic composition of the late nineteenth-century population differed vastly from that of Americans in the last thirty years of the twentieth century, both eras were characterized by one challenge after another to what were once considered settled cultural truths. The argument over the proper role of religion in civil government was (and is) only a subsidiary of the larger question of whether the claims of supposedly revealed religion deserve any particular respect or deference in a pluralistic society. The other cultural issues that divided Americans in Ingersoll's time are equally familiar and include evolution, race, immigration, women's rights, sexual behavior, freedom of artistic expression, and vast disparities in wealth. In the nineteenth century, however, the issues were newer, as was the science bolstering the secular side of the arguments, and the forces of religious orthodoxy were stronger. The overarching question in Ingersoll's time was whether any of these issues could or should be resolved by appeals to divine authority. To this Ingersoll also said no, spreading the gospel (though he would never have called it that) of reason, science, and humanism to audiences across the country. It is not an overstatement to say that Ingersoll devoted his life to freethought, the lovely term that first appeared in England in the late seventeenth century and was meant to convey devotion to a way of looking at the world based on observation rather than on ancient "sacred" writings by men who believed that the sun revolved around the earth.

Ingersoll's influence derived in part from his fulfillment of an American archetype—the self-made, self-educated man who, by his own diligence and pursuit of knowledge, rises to fame and fortune—that was already disappearing in post–Civil War America. The son of an unsuccessful Presbyterian minister who never managed to remain attached to one congregation for very long, Ingersoll grew up poor. Like his hero Abraham Lincoln, he had little formal education. Also like Lincoln, he was admitted to the bar not after studying at one of the nation's few law schools but by learning his trade—and the history and philosophy of law—in an older attorney's office on the frontier. By the time of Ingersoll's death just a year before the turn of the twentieth century, his kind of self-made American achiever—whether in law, scholarship, government, the arts, or business—was already on the way to extinction. Ingersoll spoke out of a simpler past, in which self-education was the only route to learning for those not born to money, on behalf of an American future in which education would be available to all.

Despite a schedule so demanding that he occasionally lost his voice in an era when speakers were unaided by sound amplification devices, Ingersoll transmitted energy and enthusiasm to his audiences as he walked around the stage, usually speaking from memory. Described by one twentieth-century biographer as the Babe Ruth of the podium, Ingersoll weighed more than two hundred pounds—a disproportionate share of them concentrated in his abdomen—by his forties. His portliness impelled the *Oakland Evening Tribune* to note that in another century, the amount of fat in the Great Agnostic's body would have produced a "spectacular auto da fé."[5] He told his audiences, "We are not endeavoring to chain the future, but to free the present. We are not forging fetters for our children, but we are breaking those our fathers made for us. We are the advocates of inquiry, of investigation, and thought. This of itself, is an admission that we are not perfectly satisfied with our conclusions. Philosophy has not the egotism of faith."[6] Asked if he enjoyed lecturing by a newspaper reporter in Kansas City, the ebullient Ingersoll replied, "Of course I enjoy lecturing. It is a great pleasure to drive the fiend of fear out of the hearts of men, women, and children. It is a positive joy to put out the fires of hell."[7]

The continuing lack of public consensus on the proper balance between religion and secularism in American life could easily be used to support the argument that Ingersoll's current obscurity is richly deserved. He did not, as the explosiveness of religious issues in American politics has made clear since the 1980s, put to rest the issue of whether the United States was founded as a Christian nation. Nor did he manage to lay an unshakable foundation for a future in which Americans would emphatically reject the injection of religious dogma into public schools, in which teaching the biblical story of creation in a high school biology class would be as unthinkable as telling schoolchildren that thunder and lightning were produced by Thor's hammer. Yet the persistent tension and inflamed emotion surrounding these issues—a phenomenon that exists nowhere else in the developed world—ought to enhance rather than diminish the Great Agnostic's stature. Intellectual history is a relay race, not a hundred-yard dash. Ingersoll was one of those indispensible people who keep an alternative version of history alive. Such men and women are vital to the real story and identity of a nation, because in their absence, public consensus about the past would be totally controlled by those who wish to re-create the country's mythic origins in their own image—including founder-worshippers who see the passionate risk-taking revolutionary leaders and anti-intellectual ideologues who think that too much education is a dangerous thing.

To understand Ingersoll's importance, one need only look at a partial list of distinguished Americans of his own generation who were influenced by his arguments and, even more important, younger admirers who lived on into the twentieth century to make critical contributions to American politics, science, business, and law and to become leaders on behalf of civil liberties and international human rights. This list of nineteenth- and twentieth-century luminaries—poets, artists, inventors, social reformers, even a member of the Baseball Hall of Fame—includes Clara Barton, Clarence Darrow, Luther Burbank, Eugene V. Debs, Frederick Douglass, W. C. Fields, H. L. Mencken, Robert M. LaFollette, Andrew Carnegie, Margaret Sanger, Elizabeth Cady Stanton, Mark Twain, Walt Whitman, Thomas Edison, and my favorite Ingersoll fan of all, "Wahoo" Sam Crawford, baseball's outstanding power hitter throughout the first two decades of the twentieth century.* Ingersoll's appeal as a freethinker cut across political and class boundaries. A Republican who upheld the gold standard and traveled in social circles

---

* For Crawford's memories of Ingersoll and of the early days of baseball, see Lawrence S. Ritter's *The Glory of Their Times*, chapter 4.

that included business titans like Carnegie, Ingersoll's closest friends and fervent admirers also included champions of labor such as Debs, who would garner more than a million votes as the Socialist candidate for president in 1920, and LaFollette of Wisconsin, the leader of American Progressivism until his death in 1925. "Ingersoll had a tremendous influence on me," LaFollette recalled in later years. "He liberated my mind. Freedom was what he preached; he wanted the shackles off everywhere. He wanted me to think boldly about all things. . . . He was a rare, bold, heroic figure."[8]

The nation's most famous agnostic and freethinker, also a successful trial lawyer, gave up a promising career in politics to pursue his campaign against religious orthodoxy and for the separation of church and state. Then as now, a man who openly rejected belief in a deity and in all religion could never hope to go far in American politics. As part of his mission, Ingersoll elucidated Darwin's theory of evolution for millions of Americans who might otherwise have heard about the great scientific insight of their age only through the attacks of biblical literalists. Unlike orator-celebrities today, Ingersoll did not preach only to the converted (or, in his case, to the unconverted). The diverse array of men and women who jammed lecture halls to hear Ingersoll could scarcely have presented a shaper contrast to today's segmented American audience, whose members generally tune in to pundits and log on to blogs that merely reflect and reinforce preexisting views.

Ingersoll would have been contemptuous of the idea that anonymous "free speech," as practiced by bloggers with nothing at stake in the real world, had anything of value to contribute to public discourse. To influence the public in the late nineteenth century, one was required to speak and appear as oneself. And as contemporary newspaper accounts make clear, Ingersoll was a master at reaching people who did not necessarily agree with him or who might have been downright hostile. When he appeared for the first time in medium-sized cities where orthodox religious influence was strong, Ingersoll's reputation as a heretic often held down the size of the audience. That was never true the second time the Great Agnostic spoke. Once the local newspapers reported on the entertainment value of Ingersoll's talks, tickets became a prize for scalpers. In Iowa, the *Mason City Republican* reported that a majority of those attending an 1885 Ingersoll lecture were orthodox religious believers who nevertheless appreciated Ingersoll's wit at the expense of their own faith. "Foreordination laughs jostled freewill smiles," the reporter recalled, "Baptist cachinations floated out to join apostolic roars, and there was a grand unison of orthodox cheers for the most unorthodox jokes."[9]

When Ingersoll was at the height of his career, most newspapers still followed the hoary and informative journalistic custom of reporting applause and laughter in summaries of speeches. This created something of a quandary for papers with religiously orthodox owners, because headlines reflecting the publisher's disapproval would be followed by articles detailing the audience's enjoyment of the speech. So the *New York Times* placed a headline above an account of Ingersoll's lectures at Booth's Theater announcing, "The Great Infidel Preacher Roundly Hissed"—but the subsequent article revealed that the hissing was confined to representatives of the American Bible Society, who were handing out copies of the King James version outside the theater. Quotations from the speech would be punctuated by "Great Laughter" and "Laughter, " which followed Ingersoll's description of the founding of the Church of England after Henry VIII divorced Catherine of Aragon to marry Anne Boleyn. "For awhile the new religion was regulated by law," Ingersoll remarked, "and afterward God was compelled to study acts of Parliament to find out whether a man might be saved or not. [Laughter.]"

Most satire involving contemporary events travels poorly over time, but it is not difficult to understand, after reading the basic texts of Ingersoll's lectures, why his audiences—composed not only of freethinkers but of devoted religious believers nevertheless open to skepticism about literal interpretations of the Bible—would have been charmed by his good-natured jabs. In a frequently delivered lecture titled "Some Mistakes of Moses," Ingersoll seduced his audiences by mocking the theories of a well-known theologian who, having half-digested Darwin, suggested that the serpent who deceived Eve into eating the forbidden fruit was probably a humanoid ape with the gift of speech. To the innocent Eve, the ape looked like an ordinary man (albeit a very hairy one); ergo, she was receptive to his suggestions. Subsequently, the talking ape was punished for his role in instigating original sin by being deprived of speech and condemned henceforth to the "chattering of monkeys." Ingersoll had his own take on this tortuous theological speculation. "Here then is the 'connecting link' between man and the lower creation," he explained. "The serpent was simply an orangoutang that spoke Hebrew with the greatest ease, and had the outward appearance of a perfect gentleman, seductive in manner, plausible, polite, and the most admirably calculated to deceive. It never did seem reasonable to me that a long, cold, and disgusting snake with an apple in its mouth could deceive anybody; and I am glad, even at this late date to know that the something that persuaded Eve to taste the forbidden fruit was, at least in the shape of a man."[10] A man who combined reason with humor, who drew audiences looking for entertainment along with enlightenment, was much more dangerous than someone disposed to harangue audiences with the conviction that they were simply *wrong* about what they had been taught since birth. Everyone who paid to hear Ingersoll speak knew that he or she would go away with the memory of good laughs to accompany unsettling new thoughts.

He told his audiences that when he first read *On the Origin of Species* (1859) and became acquainted with Darwin's theory of evolution, his initial reaction was to think about "how terrible this will be upon the nobility of the Old World. Think of their being forced to trace their ancestry back to the duke Orang Outang, or the princess Chimpanzee."[11] This sentence demonstrates what a brilliant orator he was, because he was taking advantage of an American hostility to Old World, and especially British, aristocracy that was much more alive in the nineteenth century than it is today. He used the American disdain for unearned hereditary privilege (which, then as now, did not necessarily extend to inherited wealth) to make the idea of descent from lower animals more accessible and less threatening. "I read about rudimentary bones and muscles," he confided. "I was told that everybody had rudimentary muscles extending from the ear into the cheek. I asked, 'What are they?' I was told: 'They are the muscles with which your ancestors used to flap their ears.' I do not

so much wonder that we had them as that we have outgrown them."[12]

Although Ingersoll opposed organized religion in general, his specific targets were believers and clerics who
wanted to impose their convictions on their fellow citizens and stifle inquiry that challenged faith. If he could
not quite convince his audiences that all religion was superstitious myth, he did convince many to seek out a form
of religion that did not require them to renounce the in-
sights of contemporary science or non-mythological history. Ingersoll himself was not much interested in debating
abstract theological or philosophical questions, although
he did so occasionally with reform-minded believers like
his good friend Henry Ward Beecher, the best-known
clerical orator of the late nineteenth century and a leader
of liberalizing forces within American Protestantism. Ingersoll was, however, interested in creating a bridge between the world of secular freethought, for which he spoke
so eloquently, and religions, including Reform Judaism
and liberal Protestant denominations, that were willing to
make room for secular knowledge (as Unitarians had in
the eighteenth century in response to Enlightenment political thought and geological discoveries that posed the
first solid scientific challenge to the biblical precept that
the earth was only four thousand years old). In this respect, Ingersoll differed significantly from those who

have been dubbed the "new atheists" in recent years and who consider "moderate" religion as bad as or worse than fundamentalism because they believe that religious moderates provide a cover that confers social respectability on all faiths.

Ingersoll himself made no distinction between atheists and agnostics. In 1885, he was asked by an interviewer for a Philadelphia newspaper, "Don't you think that the belief of the Agnostic is more satisfactory to the believer that that of the Atheist?" He replied succinctly, "The Agnostic is an Atheist. The Atheist is an Agnostic. The Agnostic says: 'I do not know; but I do not believe there is any god.' The Atheist says the same. The orthodox Christian says he knows there is a God: but we know that he does not know. The Atheist [too] cannot know that God does not exist."[13] This critical point remains a source of both confusion and willful distortion in American discourse, in large measure because the word "atheist" has a much harsher sound to American ears than the word "agnostic."* Indeed, the more equivocal, bland tone of the latter is arguably the main reason for its invention in the late nineteenth century, since atheism and atheist had long been considered extreme pejoratives.

Ingersoll frequently pointed out that the labels "atheist"

*I learned this while writing a weekly column, "The Spirited Atheist," for the *On Faith* blog published by the *Washington Post*. The emails I receive from and "infidel" had generally been applied as epithets to anyone, religious or not, who refused to accept biblical stories that were scientifically impossible. That had happened to Thomas Paine, who was also called a Judas, reptile, hog, mad dog, souse, louse, and archbeast by his religiously orthodox contemporaries. Had he done nothing else, Ingersoll's lifelong effort to restore Paine's reputation should have earned him a permanent place in American intellectual history. The future president Theodore Roosevelt dismissed Paine in 1888 as a "filthy little atheist . . . that apparently esteems a bladder of dirty water as the proper weapon with which to assail Christianity."[14] In this cultural climate, Ingersoll subtitled his standard lecture about Paine, "With His Name Left Out, The History of Liberty Cannot Be Written." He made it one of his missions not only to remind citizens in America's second century of Paine's indispensible rhetorical contributions to the revolutionary cause but to link those ideals to Paine's fierce defense of liberty of conscience and the separation of church and state.

outraged fundamentalists generally begin with an assertion that goes something like, "You claim to know that there is no God, but you have no proof. . . ." Readers who insist on calling themselves agnostics rather than atheists often voice the same misapprehension and suggest that it is "arrogant" to claim absolute knowledge of the nonexistence of a deity. But I do not claim to possess that knowledge, any more than Ingersoll or Paine did. To the fundamentalists I reply that while there is no evidentiary proof of a negative, there is also no evidentiary proof (other than inadmissible supernatural propositions) of the existence of God. To agnostics who object to the word "atheist," I suggest that they consult Ingersoll and the dictionary.

To be sure, Ingersoll achieved only partial success in his attempt to return Paine to the American historical canon. Paine's name is much better known than Ingersoll's in the United States today mainly because his role as the chief polemicist for the revolution can be described for the consumption of schoolchildren without mentioning his later accomplishments as a scourge of organized religion and a radical economic thinker. The Paine who wrote "these are the times that try men's souls" in the darkest hour for General George Washington's army is a recognizable name to a considerable number of Americans in the twenty-first century. But the Paine who wrote *The Age of Reason* (1794)—which put forth the heretical idea that the sacred books of all religions were written by human beings, not by any deity—is nearly as obscure as Ingersoll is to Americans with little interest in or knowledge about the secular side of their history.

Since no champion arose to restore Ingersoll's memory in the twentieth century as Ingersoll had once labored to revive Paine's reputation, it is not surprising that Ingersoll, who was primarily an orator even though his collected works amount to twelve volumes, is the inhabitant of a smaller historical niche than Paine today. But, contrary to the suggestions of many scholars, the ephemeral nature of oratory is not the main reason why Ingersoll is all but forgotten, just as the fact that Paine never held public office is not the main reason why there is no marble statue of him in the U.S. Capitol. The real reason why both men have been downgraded or eliminated altogether from standard school history books is their staunch and outspoken opposition to organized religion and any entanglement between religion and government. Paine, who was not in fact an atheist but a deist with religious views closely resembling those of Washington, John Adams, and Jefferson (the latter being the only one of the first three presidents to defend his old friend after publication of *The Age of Reason*), never recovered from the damage to his American reputation inflicted by the heretical book he had written in France, just before being imprisoned by the revolutionary government for his opposition to the execution of Louis XVI. Paine was destitute when he died in New York in 1809, and even the Quakers—whose religion was one of the few he admired—refused to allow him to be buried in one of their cemeteries. The anniversary of his death, marked at the time by a private burial ceremony with no family to mourn him, was observed only within the shrinking early nineteenth-century freethought community. It was a death in line with the stereotypical right-wing religious image of the fate that an agnostic or atheist deserves.

Unlike Paine, Ingersoll did not die alone and unmourned but with his wife, Eva, sitting by his bedside, after he had consumed a typically large breakfast. He also did much better financially during his lifetime than Paine, because he commanded high fees for both his legal services and his speeches—regardless of whether his audiences were scandalized or uplifted by the content. Indeed, the fact that Ingersoll made a good living out of questioning religion particularly enraged his opponents. This view is encapsulated in a cartoon, published in the satirical magazine *Puck* in 1880, showing Ingersoll beating the Bible with a stick labeled "atheism" as coins fall out of the Holy Book into the orator's briefcase. Ingersoll was, however, better at making and spending money than he was at saving, and while he did not die in debt, he left nothing like a fortune to his wife. He was fond of entertaining, and he and Eva gave legendary parties in the succession of Manhattan townhouses where they lived for the last fifteen years of Ingersoll's life. He also gave away a good deal of money away to freethought causes, the arts, and impecunious relatives and was, as he was the first to acknowledge, an inept investor. In a letter to his brother John, he wrote, "I have a positive genius for losing money."[15] Nevertheless, Ingersoll not only lived well but had, by all accounts (including his own and those of his wife and their two daughters) an extraordinarily happy marriage and family life. This abundance of creature comforts and domestic happiness did not sit well with orthodox believers, who thought that the evil of questioning the existence of God should be punished in both this life and the next. Ingersoll died in his sleep, probably of a heart attack. Every major newspaper in the country, while taking care to disavow Ingersoll's attacks on organized religion, offered extensive editorial commentaries that, more often than not, praised his personal virtues, acknowledged his influence, and regretted that he had devoted his talents to debunking religion.

Ingersoll's twelve-volume collected works were published within a few years of his death by his brother-in-law C. P. Farrell, who owned the Dresden Publishing Company (named for Ingersoll's birthplace in upstate New York). The Great Agnostic remained a well-known, frequently cited recent historical figure into the 1920s not only because many of his friends and enemies remained alive but because his writings were still thought to be capable of corrupting American youth. However, the memory of Ingersoll faded swiftly after the famous 1925 Scopes "monkey trial," which pitted the leading spokesman for religious fundamentalism, William Jennings Bryan, against Clarence Darrow, the nation's most famous criminal lawyer and an equally famous agnostic, who had been strongly influenced by hearing Ingersoll's speeches in the 1870s and 1880s. Bryan succeeded in obtaining the conviction of

John T. Scopes, a high school biology teacher in Dayton, Tennessee, on grounds of having violated a state law banning the teaching of evolution (although the verdict was reversed on appeal). But Darrow—at least in the North and among intellectuals—was thought to have been the real winner and fundamentalism the real loser after Bryan was forced to admit that even he did not take every word in the Bible literally.

That admission and the trial itself attested powerfully to the accomplishments of the freethought movement in the late nineteenth century. The Tennessee law forbidding the teaching of evolution would not have been deemed necessary by fundamentalist legislatures had evolution not made its way into high school biology textbooks by the early twentieth century. Without an orator of Ingersoll's persuasive powers to make fun of human pretensions about distinguished lineage and to humanize an idea that originally seemed so alien—that man was descended from the very creatures over whom God has supposedly given him dominion—who knows how long it would have taken for Darwin's scientific ideas to have made it into high school biology texts? In Ingersoll's era, there were other pro-evolution and pro-science speakers well known to educated Americans—most notably Thomas Henry Huxley, Darwin's close friend and the foremost international popularizer of the theory of evolution by means of natural selection (also thought to be the originator of the word "agnostic"), and Herbert Spencer, a British philosopher who coined the phrase "survival of the fittest" (often mistakenly attributed to Darwin). Spencer, who was even more influential in the United States than in England—though he is rarely read today—made the error of arguing that "survival of the fittest" could and should be applied to man in a state of civilization, thereby justifying the vast Gilded Age gap between the rich and the poor.

Although Spencer and Ingersoll were friends, Ingersoll did not make the social Darwinist mistake of believing that "tooth and claw" should be the rule in civilized societies. His rejection of social Darwinism, at a time when many freethinkers, to their discredit, shared the views of conservative religious believers about the natural inferiority of the poor, immigrants, and blacks, raises Ingersoll above most of his contemporaries in American secular thought. There are two distinct threads in the history of American secularism—the first descending from the humanism and egalitarianism of Paine and the second from nineteenth-century social Darwinism through the twentieth-century every-man-for-himself "objectivism" of Ayn Rand. A true intellectual descendant of Paine, Ingersoll linked reason and science to the success and survival of democracy, as the Enlightenment deists among the founders did, and contended that the capacity for rational thought existed among all races and social classes.

Ingersoll's belief in the intellectual potential of those at every level of society, coupled with his own modest origins, added considerable weight to the message he delivered in small towns, where farmers and baseball players were more likely to show up than university professors. Spencer's presentations certainly would not have gone over as well in Sherman, Texas, as they did in New York and Boston, given that audiences in the less culturally sophisticated towns on the frontier might have suspected that *they* would not have survived the British philosopher's social fitness test.

Looking back on the extraordinary decline in religious literalism that took place among educated Americans in the decades bracketing the turn of the century, it is easy to see why fundamentalism was prematurely declared dead by many prominent American intellectuals in the 1920s, just as the death of God would be prematurely reported in the 1960s. In 1931, the distinguished editor of *Harper's* magazine, Frederick Lewis Allen, summed up the Scopes trial in a classic work of popular history, *Only Yesterday*, that has never been out of print. "Legislators might go on passing anti-evolution laws," Allen wrote, "and in the hinterlands the pious might still keep their religion locked in a science-proof compartment of their minds; but civilized opinion everywhere had regarded the Dayton trial with amazement and amusement, and the slow drift away from Fundamentalist certainty continued."[16]

That is how things looked at the beginning of the Great Depression in the offices of prestigious magazines in New York and Boston, and that is pretty much how they would continue to look to secular intellectuals well into the 1980s. The mistaken conclusion that "science-proof" thinking would simply disappear in the enlightened twentieth century was the main factor in Ingersoll's disappearance from the consciousness of American intellectuals in the generation after his death. Ingersoll's arguments would come to seem not provocative or dangerous but irrelevant to most in the generation of historians who came of age during the Depression and the Second World War and who, like Allen, considered fundamentalism no more than an interesting relic of ages past.*

The fading-away of Ingersoll's memory seems particularly poignant at a time when American politics have confirmed the shortsightedness of those who assumed, throughout much of the twentieth century, that religion

---

*The gigantic exception to this tendency was Richard Hofstadter, whose *Social Darwinism in American Thought* (1944) and *Anti-Intellectualism in American Life* (1963) remain required reading for anyone who wishes to understand the continuing importance of the battle between religious fundamentalism and modernism in American politics.

itself was vanishing as a divisive force in American civic life. *The New York Times*, which took care to denounce Ingersoll's views about religion, nevertheless acknowledged in an editorial shortly after his death that the Great Agnostic's refusal to give up his antireligious views meant that he "never took that place in the social, the professional, or the public life of his country to which by his talents he would otherwise have been eminently entitled."[17] Edgar W. Howe, publisher of the *Atchison Daily Globe* in Kansas, expressed this view, in much more positive fashion, in a memorial editorial that spoke for freethinkers in the American heartland: "The death of Robert Ingersoll removed one of America's greatest citizens. It is not popular to admire Ingersoll but his brilliancy, his integrity and patriotism cannot be doubted. Had not Ingersoll been frank enough to express his opinions on religion, he would have been President of the United States. Hypocrisy in religion pays. There will come a time when public men may speak their honest convictions in religion without being maligned by the ignorant and superstitious, but not yet."[18]

I

The Making of an Iconoclast

Disobedience is one of the conditions of progress.
—RGI, "Individuality"

In the tiny town of Dresden, near the shore of Lake Seneca in upstate New York, stands the modest frame house in which Robert Ingersoll was born. The Ingersoll Birthplace Museum, operated by the Council for Secular Humanism, houses the memorabilia of a lifetime dedicated to the cause of freethought. The collection contains mementos ranging from a scratchy recording Ingersoll made in his friend Thomas Edison's laboratory in Menlo Park, New Jersey, to a Yiddish translation of his lecture "Some Mistakes of Moses," indicating that freethinking Jewish immigrants on New York's Lower East Side were as attuned to the Great Agnostic's message as American-born expatriates from Christianity. Supported by a small number of donors, the facility attracts only the most devout freethought enthusiasts, partly because it lacks the digital paraphernalia considered essential for the expansion of museum audiences and partly because of its off-the-beaten-track location. Although the area is spectacularly beautiful, with crystalline lakes (known as the Finger Lakes because of their shape) formed more than two million years ago by glaciers during the Ice Age, it is at least a five-hour drive from any major population center in the Northeast. But the Ingersoll museum's obscurity in the tourist landscape has less to do with its location or its antiquated paper-and-ink aura (which can be an advantage for small historic houses) than with the general lack of public knowledge about America's secular freethought traditions. Only an hour's drive away in Seneca Falls, the National Women's Hall of Fame, founded in 1969, offers visitors a technologically up-to-date experience in the town where Elizabeth Cady Stanton and Lucretia Mott launched the nineteenth-century woman suffrage movement with a declaration that "all men and women are created equal."* The feminist movement has done a much more effective job of reclaiming its own history, and of garnering donations, than the growing number of Amer-

*The Seneca Falls *Declaration of Rights and Sentiments* was written by Stanton, in consultation with Mott, at her kitchen table and was modeled after the Declaration of Independence and the American Anti-Slavery Association's founding document, written in 1833 by William Lloyd Garrison and titled *Declaration of Sentiments*.

ican secularists have of preserving and publicizing their heritage. The proportion of Americans who are unaffiliated with any religion and who consider their outlook on public affairs wholly or predominantly secular has doubled during the past two decades, but this decline in religious faith does not necessarily translate into a commitment to the promotion of secular values or knowledge of secular American history and its heroes.*

The future scourge of orthodox clerics was born on August 11, 1833, to the Reverend John Ingersoll, a Presbyterian minister, and his wife, Mary Livingston Ingersoll.† Although the Finger Lakes area was predominantly agricultural, it also participated in the late 1820s and 1830s in the new commercial prosperity generated by the Erie Canal, which opened in 1825, connecting the Great Lakes to the Hudson River and therefore to New York City and Europe. The canal was the greatest engineering feat of the first half of the American nineteenth century and served as the vital connection between the western frontier and the eastern seaboard for most of the 1800s.

---

*The increase in the number of Americans who do not belong to any church and who consider their outlook on public affairs wholly or predominantly secular was first reported in the *American Religious Identification Survey* conducted by the City University of New York in 2001. The trend has continued during the past decade.

† Ingersoll's mother, who died when he was only two and a half years old, was a collateral descendent of the prominent New York revolutionary figure Robert R. Livingston, who administered the oath of office to George Washington in 1789, when New York City was the nation's capital.

Without the Erie Canal, it would have taken much longer for the young American republic to exploit the politically imaginative leap of the Louisiana Purchase. This first great achievement of American technology fueled the ambition of and created liberating possibilities for a generation that came of age when the manmade waterway was crucial to the economic development of a westward-expanding nation—just as the automobile, a century later, would encourage personal mobility on a previously unimagined scale.

Another characteristic of the Finger Lakes region was its wide variety of dissident religious and social movements, and that cultural history makes it seem almost providential that Ingersoll was born there. Although his family moved away from Dresden when Robert was less than a year old, the social ferment for which the region was widely known—especially an ongoing conflict between abolitionism and those who favored continuing toleration of slavery in order to preserve the Union—certainly helped shape the outlook of his parents. The entire area was known as the "burned-over district," because it was said that various religious revival movements, as well as secular dissident impulses, swept through the region like wildfires. A partial list of religious and political iconoclasts who either were born in the Finger Lakes region or were intimately linked to the area's varied dissident impulses includes Elizabeth Cady Stanton, the founding mother of the nineteenth-century woman suffrage movement; Amelia Jencks Bloomer, the inventor and popularizer of the eponymous pantaloons and editor of the first American newspaper aimed specifically at women; Harriet Tubman, the heroic slave-rescuer known as the "Moses of her people"; and, at a distinctly different place on the religio-political spectrum, the Mormon founding father Joseph Smith, who walked into a forest one day and walked out with golden tablets, presented by the angel Moroni, upon which the Book of Mormon was supposedly inscribed.

The original English-speaking settlers of the area came from New England and included both orthodox Presbyterians and Congregationalists and nonconformist Protestants, among them Quakers, Unitarians, and Universalists. Quakers were, of course, the most staunch religious opponents of slavery. One myth of American religious history maintains that most northern churches took a strong abolitionist stance on moral grounds long before the Civil War. In fact, the more religiously orthodox and socially conservative Protestant denominations, including Presbyterians and Congregationalists, were much more concerned in the 1830s and 1840s with maintaining the unity of churches in the North and the South than with limiting or abolishing slavery. John Ingersoll, however, was first and foremost a fiery abolitionist preacher. His message did not always sit well in an area that, like much of New York State, was highly ambivalent about slavery. One of Lake Seneca's tourist attractions today, just a fifteen-minute drive from Ingersoll's native hamlet and the site of his father's church, is the Greek revival Rose Hill Mansion, built by Robert Selden Rose, a Virginia planter who arrived in 1802 with twenty-six slaves. Rose's slaves were freed only in 1827, when the "peculiar institution" was finally abolished in New York State.*

The elder Ingersoll (also known, strangely for a Protestant, as Priest Ingersoll) was in the habit of describing the South as an "earthly Gehenna"—and that may not have pleased Dresden parishioners in the 1830s, given that they had tolerated an imported piece of that Gehenna just down the road throughout the first quarter of the nineteenth century.[1] Ingersoll's mother also took a public abolitionist stand, not long after New York finally abolished slavery, by circulating a state petition to Congress that the practice be outlawed in the District of Columbia. At the time, women—especially not preacher's wives expected to serve as models of Christian propriety—

---

*The history of slavery in areas where it was practiced in the North can be even touchier than it is in the South. When I toured Rose Hill, which has been restored by the Geneva Historical Society, in 2001, the guide did not mention that David Selden Rose was a slaveholder. Only when I returned to New York City and began doing some background research in the History and Genealogy section of the New York Public Library did I discover that this had been a plantation in every historical sense of the word.

rarely took such public action. According to one of Ingersoll's early biographers, Mary Ingersoll's behavior "aroused
comment in New York that had been not always kind, for
that state ... admiring good women, none the less preferred them not overly intelligent and inaudible."[2] Although Robert was too young when his mother died for
him to remember her when he grew up, he was aware not
only that she had been an abolitionist but that she had
acted on her convictions at a time when it was considered
scandalous for women to openly involve themselves in
public affairs. This awareness may well have contributed to
Ingersoll's lifelong advocacy of equal rights for women—a
cause that received considerable lip service from but was
rarely a priority for male freethinkers.

Throughout Robert's childhood, his father's outspoken
abolitionist views were a major factor in the peripatetic
nature of his clerical career. Frequent moves suggest that
Priest Ingersoll must have encountered trouble with the
vestrymen in one congregation after another, because this
was an era when successful clergymen often remained in
one parish for life. He left Dresden in 1834 to take up the
post of assistant pastor at a new Presbyterian church on
Broadway in New York City, but that job lasted less than a
year. The problem in New York was definitely Ingersoll's
unrestrained abolitionism. When the Broadway church
had been under construction, an angry crowd set fire to

the partly built structure because "they had heard that miscegenation was about to be championed."[3] When one considers that slavery had been outlawed for less than a decade, it is not surprising that New Yorkers would fail to take kindly to a preacher who told them that they had only recently been engaged in committing a grievous sin. So the die-hard abolitionist moved back the town of Cazenovia in upstate New York, where his wife died in 1835, leaving five children behind. Mary's death, at age thirty-six, was not at all unusual for a mother of her generation, in which the physical complications attendant upon repeated childbearing prevented many women from living long enough to raise their families.

What little we know about Ingersoll's childhood comes from his own recollections in speeches and later family correspondence. Because of Priest Ingersoll's frequent moves in search of new congregations, the family was always economically insecure. Robert's older sisters, Ruth and Mary, were expected, as was customary in such families, to fill in for their dead mother by looking after the younger children. Robert was closest to his brother, Ebon Clark, who was just two years older. After their mother's death, Robert and Ebon—who was always called Clark by his brothers and sisters—became inseparable; they shared a special, intimate language (a phenomenon more common in twins) that no one else could understand. Ebon, who grew up to become a congressman from Illinois, was the only one of the Ingersoll children who would share his brother's antireligious views in adulthood. His other brother, John, and his sisters—with whom he remained on good terms throughout his life—were, as the family correspondence indicates, orthodox in their religious beliefs.

The theological cast of the Ingersoll home, coupled with a catch-as-catch-can exposure to formal education necessitated by his father's wandering ministry, had the opposite effect on the two younger boys. Robert and Ebon were rarely enrolled in school for any length of time—a background they shared with many other American autodidacts, including Abraham Lincoln, who lived in small towns or rural frontier areas in the first half of the nineteenth century. They were, however, exposed to a surfeit of religious reading. Their father, who had prepared for the ministry at Middlebury College in Vermont, kept mainly religious books in the house—the King James Bible, naturally; Foxe's famous, gory *Book of Martyrs*; Richard Baxter's *The Saint's Everlasting Rest*, William Paley's *Moral and Political Philosophy* and *Evidences*; the eighteenth-century Methodist theologian Richard Sibbes's interestingly titled *Believers' Bowels Opened*; John Bunyan's *Pilgrim's Progress*; and the works of John Milton. As an adult, Ingersoll underestimated Milton, who was far too great a poet not to make Satan the most unforgettable character he ever met. The Great Agnostic could not see beyond the Puritan to the genius of the poetry, which he described as the sum of "all the sublime absurdities that religion wrought with the blind man's brain."[4]

Like many an atheist or agnostic before and after him, Ingersoll developed an early skepticism about religion precisely because he was exposed to so many religious books at a young age. Listen to him eviscerate Paley's "watchmaker" argument in *Evidences*, which Ingersoll must have read at some point in his father's library in the 1840s and is still used by the proponents of "intelligent design" as an argument that the universe could not have evolved randomly but must have been planned by a creator.

A man finds a watch and it is so wonderful that he concludes that it must have had a maker. He finds the maker and he is so much more wonderful than the watch that he says he must have had a maker. Then he finds God, the maker of the man, and he is so much more wonderful than the man that he could not have had a maker. This is what the lawyers call a departure in pleading.

According to Paley there can be no design without a designer—but there can be a designer without design. The wonder of the watch suggested the watchmaker, and the wonder of the watchmaker suggested the creator, and the wonder of the creator demonstrated that he was not created—but was uncaused and eternal.[5]

For an inquisitive child steeped in religious reading, there would have been nothing but questions as a result of his early, narrow, but intense self-education. Ingersoll would also recall the scholarship of Adam Clarke, another Methodist biblical commentator, as the work of one who "thought that the serpent seduced our mother Eve, and was in fact the father of Cain. He also believed that the animals, while in the ark, had their natures changed to that degree that they devoured straw together and enjoyed each other's society—thus prefiguring the blessed millennium."[6]

It would often be suggested by Ingersoll's critics that his antireligious stance was the result of a particularly harsh upbringing by his severe preacher-father. He denied this strongly and repeatedly described his father as a victim of cruel religious teachings that corrupted normal family relations. "My father was a man of great natural tenderness," Ingersoll wrote, "and loved his children almost to insanity. The little severity he had was produced by his religion. Like most men of his time, he thought Solomon knew something about raising children. For my part, I think he should have known better than to place

the least confidence in the advice of a man so utterly idi-
otic as to imagine he could be happy with seven hundred
wives."[7] It would have been surprising if "Priest Ingersoll," however tender his feelings toward his children, had
not used the rod and the belt to punish them from time
to time. Corporal punishment, at home and school, was
widely accepted by Americans of all social classes and
most religions. The morality of beating one's children
was never questioned by those who adhered to a literal
interpretation of the Bible.

As an adult champion of freethought, Ingersoll would
express his detestation of corporal punishment repeatedly
in speeches dealing with family relations and the rights of
women and children. By then, he would strike a respon-
sive chord not only among freethinkers but among liberal
Christians, who disagreed with the harsh biblical philosophy of punishment advocated by fundamentalists. "Do
you know," Ingersoll asked his audiences, "that I have
seen some people who acted as though they thought when
the Savior said, 'Suffer the little children to come unto
me, for of such is the kingdom of heaven,' he had a raw-
hide under his mantle and made that remark simply to
get the children within striking distance?" Ingersoll suggested that parents have a picture taken of themselves
while in the act of whipping their children. "I want you to
have a photograph . . . when you are in the act, with your

face red with vulgar anger, and the face of the little child, with eyes swimming in tears and the little chin dimpled with fear, like a piece of water struck by a sudden cold wind."[8] Ingersoll's argument against corporal punishment paralleled his opposition to both slavery and capital punishment: He insisted that all of these practices degraded those who imposed them even more than they did the victims. (Opposition to the death penalty was common, although not universal, among freethinkers. It should be recalled that Thomas Paine placed his own life in danger when, while living in Paris, he opposed the execution of King Louis XVI. Paine was arrested in December 1793 on the personal orders of Robespierre and then spent nine months in Luxembourg Prison before the American government pressured the French to release him. En route to jail, he had managed to deliver the just-completed manuscript of Part 1 of *The Age of Reason* to his friend Joel Barlow, who was also a close friend of Thomas Jefferson's.)

Even if Ingersoll's father was not a particularly harsh parent by mid-nineteenth-century standards, young Bob's status as a "preacher's kid" certainly exposed him to the most dreary, confining practices and tenets of the most orthodox form of contemporary American religion. In one of his most popular lectures, "The Liberty of Man, Woman, and Child," Ingersoll offered a detailed description of a typical Sabbath in a minister's household. He recalled that "no matter how cold the weather was, there was no fire in the church. It was thought to be a kind of sin to be comfortable while you were thanking God. The first church that ever had a stove in it in New England divided on that account."

After the opening sermon "came the catechism with the chief end of man. We went through with that. The minister asked us if we knew that we all deserved to go to hell if it was God's will, and every little liar shouted 'Yes.'" When the service, which lasted nearly all morning, was finally over, the Ingersoll children were allowed to go home, and "if we had been good boys, and the weather was warm, sometimes they would take us out to the graveyard to cheer us up a little. It did cheer me. When I looked at the sunken tombs and the leaning stones, and read the half-effaced inscriptions through the moss of silence and forgetfulness, it was a great comfort. The reflection came to my mind that the observance of the Sabbath could not last always." Ingersoll cited a well-known Protestant hymn that looks forward to an afterlife *where congregations ne'er break up / And Sabbaths never end.* He concluded, "These lines, I think, prejudiced me a little even against heaven." Ingersoll's audiences would laugh uproariously at his description of playing in the graveyard as a Sunday treat.

A turning point in Ingersoll's development was his discovery, in adolescence, of the classics of western literature and of the poetry and prose that sprang from the Enlightenment. Being raised "respectably," Ingersoll said, meant that he was supposed to read "only such books as would start you in the narrow road for the New Jerusalem."[9] His acquaintance with Shakespeare began only in his teens, when he started traveling by himself and looking for work while his father was trying unsuccessfully to find an ecclesiastical home in Illinois. Ingersoll's description of hearing Shakespeare read aloud for the first time is worth quoting in full, because it captures the thrill of discovery that is the essence of true learning and is so frequently smothered, or forgotten, in the course of a formal education that now takes place within institutions. Ingersoll was speaking in 1895, at the height of his fame as an orator, after a dinner in honor of Anton Seidl, conductor of the New York Philharmonic Orchestra.

> But one night I stopped at a little hotel in Illinois, many years ago, when we were not quite civilized, when the footsteps of the red man were still on the prairies. While I was waiting for supper an old man was reading from a book, and among others who were listening was myself. I was filled with wonder.

I had never heard anything like it. I was ashamed to ask him what he was reading; I supposed that an intelligent boy ought to know. So I waited, and when the little bell rang for supper I hung back and they went out. I picked up the book; it was Sam Johnson's edition of Shakespeare. The next day I bought a copy for four dollars. My God! More than the national debt. You talk about the present straits of the Treasury! For days, for nights, for months, for years, I read those books, two volumes, and I commenced with the introduction. I haven't read that introduction for nearly fifty years, certainly forty-five, but I remember it still. Other writers are like a garden diligently planted and watered, but Shakespeare a forest where the oaks and elms toss their branches to the storm, where the pine towers, where the vine bursts into blossoms at its foot. That book opened to me a new world, another nature. . . . That book has been a source of perpetual joy to me from that day to this; and whenever I read Shakespeare—if it ever happens that I fail to find some new beauty, some new presentation of some wonderful truth, or another word that bursts into blossom, I shall make up my mind that my mental faculties are failing, that it is not the fault of the book.[10]

What is striking about this description (apart from a lack of critical self-consciousness, which would prevent a speaker today from comparing a writer's work to a mighty oak or a flowering vine) is its unabashed joy. The parallels with Lincoln, another self-educated devotee of both Shakespeare and Enlightenment reason, are equally striking. Ingersoll encountered religious writings in childhood, but Lincoln, born in 1809 to an illiterate father, was taught to read by his mother and had access in his early years to only the Bible and a rudimentary speller. Lincoln likely discovered Shakespeare through an edition of William Scott's eighteenth-century anthology *Lessons in Elocution, Or, A Selection of Pieces, in Prose and Verse*, brought into the household by his stepmother, Sarah Bush Lincoln, when she married Abraham's father in 1820. He did not acquire his own complete edition of Shakespeare until later in life, but Scott's anthology contains fifteen dialogues and soliloquies from eight plays. Like Ingersoll, Lincoln related to Shakespeare as much through imagined sound as through the playwright's characters and ideas. Only after he moved to Washington as a congressman in 1847 (for just one term) did Lincoln have the chance to see Shakespeare's plays performed regularly, and he often said that he preferred the sound of Shakespeare in his own head to the lines as delivered by professional actors.

Although Ingersoll was twenty-four years younger than Lincoln, both men spent their childhoods in an America far removed from the proliferation of instruments of communication and entertainment that characterized the Gilded Age. When Lincoln and Ingersoll were children, there was little competition (unless you were devoutly religious and entranced by church services and clerical oratory) for the intellectual and emotional space occupied by the printed word. To grow up before routine use of the telegraph, before the rise of the mass-circulation newspaper, before photography, before railroads linked every part of the continent was the equivalent of growing up in the twentieth century before television and, later, before the personal computer. Lincoln lived (barely) into the new era of nineteenth-century mass communication; Ingersoll, however, was a master not only of oratory but of all the Gilded Age methods of publicizing the ideas he delivered in his lectures.

The spoken and written word were much closer to each other in the first than in the second half of the nineteenth century. Ingersoll's and Lincoln's favorite poet—the English-language poet most revered by late eighteenth-, nineteenth-, and early twentieth-century freethinkers—was Robert Burns (1759–1796), whose lyrics were sung as often as they were read. Walt Whitman would later join

Burns in Ingersoll's personal pantheon of freethinking writers, but Burns was the poet who most influenced him in his youth. Between modern readers and Burns—to the extent that he is still read—stands a barrier created not only by his use of Scottish dialect but by the association of some of his best-known lyrics with songs so popular (*Auld Lang Syne, My Love Is Like a Red, Red Rose*) for so many generations that the lyrics themselves now seem hackneyed. Ingersoll also appreciated Byron, Shelley, and Keats, who, like Burns, were embraced by other nineteenth-century freethinkers, but it is easy to see in retrospect why the son of the Scottish Enlightenment occupied a special place in both the hearts and brains of the religiously unorthodox. Burns was an erotic poet and a love poet, a celebrant of nature who appealed to both early nineteenth-century Romantics and late nineteenth-century advocates of Darwin's theory of evolution. Last but not least, especially for freethinkers, Burns was a fiercely anti-clerical and anti-Calvinist thinker who accepted no distinction between satire and blasphemy. In "Holy Willie's Prayer," he offered a parody of Calvin's theory of predestination and divine intercession that freethinkers in the next century, on both sides of the Atlantic, could (as Ingersoll sometimes did) recite word for word even if they could not reproduce the Scottish dialect.

I

O Thou that in the Heavens does dwell,
Wha, as it pleases best Thysel
Sends ane to Haaven and an' to Hell
    A' for Thy glory,
And no for onie guid or ill
    They've done before Thee!

II

I bless and praise Thy matchless might.
When thousands Thou has left in night,
That I am here before Thy sight
    For gifts an' grace
A burning and a shining light
    To a' this place.

IV

When from my mither's womb I fell,
Thou might have plunged me into hell
To gnash my gooms, and weep, and wail
    In Burning lakes,
Where damned devils roar and yell,
    Chain'd to their stakes.

V

Yet I am here, a chosen sample,
To show Thy grace is great and ample,

I'm here a pillar o' Thy temple,
Strong as a rock,
A guide, a buckler, and example
To a' Thy flock!

Ingersoll's reading of religious books in a minister's household and his discovery of secular literature and infidel thought in adolescence were his formative intellectual influences. Outside of his reading, the most significant social and political influence on Ingersoll's development was his coming of age at a time when the fatal flaw in the nation's foundation, slavery, was becoming an unbridgeable chasm. Southern Illinois, where Ingersoll prepared for his career as a lawyer under the tutelage of older attorneys (as Lincoln had a generation earlier) was, in many respects, a crucible of the tensions and passions—involving race, religion, and social and economic mobility—that would soon explode into Civil War and would continue to ignite debate throughout the rest of the nineteenth century. When Ingersoll's father took his ministry to Illinois in the early 1850s, he could hardly have picked an area of the country, outside the slave states of the Deep South, where an uncompromising abolitionist clergyman would be less welcome.

The slavery issue and the Civil War shaped the lifelong politics and passions of Ingersoll's generation throughout the divided nation. Nowhere was this more true than in border areas just north and south of the Mason-Dixon line. Southern Illinois, like the southernmost counties of Ohio and Indiana, had many settlers who not only approved of slavery but had relatives in the South who owned slaves. The infamous Fugitive Slave Act of 1850, which required residents of non-slave states to assist slave owners attempting to recapture their fleeing "property" in the North, had considerable support in areas where members of the same family might, thanks to arbitrary state lines, live in different rooms of the house divided. In all of the counties where Ingersoll lived in his early twenties, gangs of "man-stealers," as they were called by those who opposed slavery, were active in seeking out escaped slaves and returning them to their former owners for a handsome fee.

In 1854, the year Ingersoll and his brother, Ebon Clark, were admitted to the bar, the Kansas-Nebraska Act decreed that settlers of each territory could decide for themselves whether they wanted to legalize slavery. The area was as bitterly divided over slavery as neighboring Missouri and Kansas, where savage guerrilla warfare between northern and southern sympathizers would take the lives of thousands of civilians during the Civil War. In the town of Marion, where Ingersoll and his brother read law before their admission to the bar, young men joined together to ride over to Kansas and establish temporary homes so that they could cast their votes for a pro-slavery legislature. Ingersoll actually began his political life as a "Stephen Douglas Democrat"—someone opposed to slavery but willing to allow new states, like Kansas, to work out their own solutions through popular elections.* But as it became clear that the South not only would pursue its slaves if they tried to escape to the North but was bent on the extension of slavery into new American territory, Ingersoll came to agree with Lincoln that the nation could not continue to exist half-slave and half-free. During the 1860 election, when Ingersoll ran unsuccessfully as a Democrat for Congress—his first and only political candidacy—he sealed his fate by delivering a stinging attack on the Fugitive Slave Act at Galesburg, a station on the Underground Railroad. Ingersoll declared the law "the most infamous enactment that ever disgraced a statute book." The act, he said, forced the entire American public to participate in a crime—that of treating their fellow men as property to be returned to owners.[11]

By the time Fort Sumter was attacked in 1861, Ingersoll no longer had a place in the Democratic Party. He

---

*The extension of slavery into new territories was the crux of the famous 1858 debates between Lincoln and the incumbent Illinois senator Stephen A. Douglas. Although Douglas won the Illinois election, the debates, which were widely publicized and reprinted throughout the country, catapulted Lincoln to national prominence and launched his campaign for the presidency in 1860.

joined the Union Army as a colonel (a title by which he was addressed for the rest of his life) and commander of the 111th Regiment, Illinois Volunteer Cavalry. Just a year later, Ingersoll was captured by the forces of General Nathan Bedford Forrest at Clifton, Tennessee, and paroled—allowed to return to the North—four days later. (At that point in the conflict, for reasons that belong in a military history of the Civil War, the release and repatriation of officers on both sides was a common practice.) In June of that year, Ingersoll resigned his commission and returned to his wife, Eva, whom he had married just after beginning his military service.

Ingersoll had not been an enthusiastic soldier, and it seems unlikely that he would ever have participated in a war that did not involve issues as important as slavery and the preservation of the Union. Shortly after the Battle of Shiloh, in a letter to his brother Ebon, he scoffed at exaggerated reports of military heroism. "I have seen flaming accounts of skirmishes in which I was engaged myself, and ninety-nine hundredths was a regular lie and the other hundredth stretched like damnation . . . if lying will get a name in the papers, there will be but few left out."[12] Years and even decades after Ingersoll's death, when clerical enemies were still trying to sully his memory by claiming that he had been a coward on the battlefield, various publications sought out Confederate veterans to talk about

Ingersoll's four days in Confederate captivity. "Ingersoll made a good fight," said one. "It was enough to make a Christian of him but it did not. His famous lectures years after show that while we did not convert him, he loved everybody during the rest of his life, and if he really believed there is no hell we convinced him that there was something mighty like it."[13]

Shortly after the war, and long before he became a national figure, Ingersoll began to link slavery with retrograde religion in his public speeches. While giving full credit to devoutly religious abolitionists like William Lloyd Garrison and Wendell Phillips, Ingersoll pointed out to his audiences that these men had been exceptions among their religious contemporaries in the North and that religious opponents of slavery had often been denounced by orthodox clerics as infidels. In a powerful speech titled "Address to the Colored People" and delivered in 1867 in Galesburg, Ingersoll declared that "the great argument of slaveholders in all countries has been that slavery is a divine institution, and thus stealing human beings has always been fortified with a, 'Thus saith the Lord.'"[14] Many defenders of slavery, Ingersoll noted, had rationalized the institution on grounds that it served to "Christianize" the Negro. He cited the Quaker abolitionist poet John Greenleaf Whittier's famous lines about a preacher who "Bade the slave-ship speed from coast to coast / Fanned by the wings of the Holy Ghost."*

Although Ingersoll had already established a reputation as a brilliant courtroom orator while pursuing his political ambitions in the Illinois Republican Party, the Galesburg speech clearly demonstrated the connection between Ingersoll's antireligious stance and his views on public policy. He refused to go along with the postbellum rewriting of history, which maintained that northern religion was unified in its support for abolition and has survived to this day as the standard viewpoint in American elementary and secondary school history textbooks. "The word Liberty is not in any [religious] creed in the world," Ingersoll told the Galesburg audience, which must have included many born into slavery. "Slavery is right according to the law of man, shouted the judge. It is right according to the law of God, shouted the priest. Thus sustained by what they were pleased to call the law of God and man, slaveholders never voluntarily freed the slaves, with the exception of the Quakers."[15]

It is somewhat mystifying that both the content and

---

*In "The Preacher," one of Whittier's many well-known antislavery poems, the lines quoted by Ingersoll are followed by: *And begged for the love of Christ, the gold, / Coined from the hearts in its groaning hold. / What could it matter, more or less / Of strikes, and hunger, and weariness? / Living or dying, bond or free / What was time to eternity?*

date of the Galesburg speech have been largely overlooked by Ingersoll's biographers, because it indicates that Ingersoll—even when he still had hope of holding public office—was unable or unwilling to take the politically prudent step of muting his antireligious views. Having been appointed state attorney general in 1867 by the Republican governor of Illinois, Ingersoll sought—and failed—to obtain the party's nomination for the governorship in 1868. His reputation as a religious skeptic was already established in Illinois (though not yet nationally) because of remarks like those in his address at Galesburg. In 1882, Ingersoll would look back on his unsuccessful bid for the Illinois governorship in a series of interviews responding to the hostile commentaries of the Reverend Thomas DeWitt Talmage, a prominent Presbyterian minister second only to Henry Ward Beecher as a renowned clerical orator of that period. "Mr. Talmage says that Christianity must be true, because an infidel cannot be elected to office," Ingersoll noted. "Now, suppose that enough infidels should happen to settle in one precinct to elect one of their own number to office; would that prove that Christianity was *not* true in that precinct?"[16] Talmage had argued that the inability of any American who disavowed belief in God to be elected to high office proved the truth of Christianity, and he used Ingersoll's defeat for the gubernatorial nomination as an example. To this Ingersoll replied:

> I presume that Mr. Talmage really thinks that I was extremely foolish to avow my real opinions. . . . But I was an infidel, and admitted it. Surely, I should not be held in contempt by Christians for having made the admission. I was not a believer in the Bible, and I said so. I was not a Christian, and I said so. I was not willing to receive the support of any man under a false impression. . . . According to the ethics of Mr. Talmage I made a mistake, and this mistake is brought forward as another evidence of the inspiration of the Scriptures. If I had only been elected Governor of Illinois,—that is to say, if I had been a successful hypocrite, I might now be basking in the sunshine of this gentleman's respect. . . . There are many men now in office who, had they pursued a nobler course, would be private citizens. Nominally, they are Christians; actually, they are nothing; and this is the combination that generally insures political success.[17]

It is worth noting that Ingersoll's last observation remains true at the national level today, although nominal Jews have also entered the ranks of the politically acceptable. Only one congressman, Democratic Representative Pete

Stark of California, is a self-acknowledged, unapologetic atheist, although there are now a fair number of legislators in the House and Senate who, practicing their own version of "don't ask, don't tell," simply avoid discussing their religious beliefs in public. Ingersoll was not even willing to remain silent.

I I

The Political Insider and the Religious Outsider

I believe that this realm of thought is not a democracy,
where the majority rule; it is not a republic. It is a
country with one inhabitant.
    —RGI, "The Limits of Toleration"

The rejection of nominal Christianity as a cover for private agnosticism would shape Robert Ingersoll's entire public life after his failure to obtain the Republican nomination for the Illinois governorship. From the perspective of twenty-first-century American politics, however, one of the most curious aspects of Ingersoll's subsequent career was his success at building and maintaining national influence within the Republican Party even as his open disavowal of religion ruled him out both as a viable candidate and, later, as a suitable nominee for high appointive office. In the late 1860s and early 1870s, Ingersoll—not yet a national figure—began to deliver heretical lectures throughout the Middle West. This group of early speeches, which he would expand on throughout the nation at the height of his career in the 1880s and 1890s, included a tribute to German naturalist and explorer Alexander von Humboldt (1869), an homage to Thomas Paine (1870), an indictment of supernaturalism in all forms (1872), and an appreciation of heretics condemned by theocracies (1874). There could be little doubt about Ingersoll's general stance on religion, including orthodox Christianity, when, in his 1872 lecture "The Gods," he noted that man-created deities "have demanded the most abject and degrading obedience" and that to please such gods, "man must lay his very face in the dust." Naturally, Ingersoll observed, the gods "have always been partial to the people who created them, and have generally shown their partiality by assisting those people to rob and destroy others, and to ravish their wives and daughters."[1]

Ingersoll's views about religion were well known not only to his regional audiences but to national Republican leaders, who were acquainted with him through both his political speeches and his successful legal representation of many corporate clients, including railroads, with close ties to the party in the era of expanding industrial capitalism after the Civil War. Ingersoll had even stronger links to Republicans who had joined the party during the early years of its formation, in opposition to slavery and to southern secession. None of these associations, however, fully explain why Republican candidates who ostensibly respected religion were eager for the endorsement of an antireligious orator.

First and foremost, Ingersoll's oratorical gifts, according to contemporary accounts, were incomparable. He was not a national figure until, in June 1876, he nominated James G. Blaine for the presidency at the Republican convention in Cincinnati. This became known as the "Plumed Knight" speech after Ingersoll declared, "Like an armed warrior, like a plumed knight, James G. Blaine marched down the halls of the American Congress and thrust his shining lance full and fair against the brazen foreheads of the defamers of his country and the maligners of his honor. For the Republican party to desert this gallant leader now, is as though an army should desert their general on the field of battle."[2] (As a member of Congress in the 1860s, Blaine had been associated with charges of corruption in the awarding of railroad contracts. No criminal wrongdoing was ever proved, but the lingering scent of scandal was enough to give Rutherford B. Hayes the nomination.) Ingersoll's speech, however, endowed the orator with a national prominence that he would never lose. The day after Ingersoll's nominating address, the *Chicago Times* described his oratory on behalf of Blaine as "the passionately dramatic scene of the day." In the florid prose characteristic of contemporary press accounts of major public events, the newspaper declared that Ingersoll "had half won his audience before he spoke a word" and delivered a speech more brilliant than any ever seen at an American political convention. "The matchless measure of the man [Ingersoll] can never be imagined from the report in type," the decidedly non-objective article continued. "To realize the prodigious force, the inexpressible power, the irrestrainable fervor of the audience requires actual sight. Words can do but meagre justice to the wizard power of this extraordinary man. He swayed and moved and impelled and restrained and worked in all ways with the mass before him as if he possessed some key to the innermost mechanism that moves the human heart, and when he finished, his fine, frank face as calm as when he began, the overwrought thousands sank back in an exhaustion of unspeakable wonder and delight."[3] You had to be there, I guess—especially since Ingersoll's oratory did not sway enough delegates to win Blaine the nomination.* But the newspaper was accurate in its description of the emerging consensus about Ingersoll as the most compelling orator of his era. As the authors of a definitive history of nineteenth- and early twentieth-century American oratory would drily observe in 1943, "There was apparently an infectious quality in Ingersoll's eloquence that tinc-

---

*Many historians have suggested that Franklin D. Roosevelt used Ingersoll's "Plumed Knight" speech as the model for his 1928 "Happy Warrior" speech nominating New York's governor Al Smith as the Democratic presidential candidate in 1928.

tured even the reports of newspapermen who covered his speeches. . . . If even half the stories of his charm are true, it must have been very difficult for any audience that had fallen under the true spell of his geniality to disagree with him."[4] Mark Twain, a much more shrewd and skeptical observer than any newspaper reporter of his era, fell under the Great Agnostic's spell in 1879 (the two had not yet met and become friends) when he first heard Ingersoll speak at a convention of veterans of the Grand Army of the Republic. "He was to respond to the toast of 'The Volunteers,'" Twain would recall, "and his first sentence or two showed his quality. As his third sentence fell from his lips the house let go with a crash. . . . Presently, when Ingersoll came to the passage in which he said that these volunteers had shed their blood and perilled their lives in order that a mother might own her own child, the language was so fine, whatever it was, for I have forgotten, and the delivery was so superb that the vast multitude wrote as one man and stood on their feet, shouting, stamping, and filling all the place with such a waving of napkins that it was like a snow storm."[5]

A second, albeit also secondary, factor in Ingersoll's influence as a Republican mover-and-shaker was the presence of many more freethinkers—even if they did not publicly acknowledge their religious skepticism and remained nominal Christians—among Republicans than among

Democrats. The party of Lincoln was also the party most closely associated with respect for contemporary science, liberalizing trends within Protestantism, and the separation of church and state. Lincoln himself never joined a church, before or after becoming president, and he was so cagy about any public revelation of his religious views that nearly every American group of religious believers and religious skeptics has, at some point, tried to claim the martyred leader as its own.* In addition to his well-known admiration for such writers as Shakespeare, Byron, and Burns, all enshrined in the freethought pantheon, Lincoln was also influenced as a young man by Paine's *The Age of Reason* and the French Enlightenment philosopher Constantin Volney's *The Ruins.*† A more persuasive argument on behalf of Lincoln as a religious skeptic than his reading were his repeated rejections, as president, of

---

*Hundreds of books have been devoted solely to analyzing the purported religious, or antireligious, beliefs of Lincoln. Even a glancing survey makes clear the lack of agreement about the sixteenth president's true views: *Abraham Lincoln, the Ideal Christian* (1913); *Lincoln the Freethinker* (1924); *Abraham Lincoln and Hillel's Golden Rule* (1929); *Abraham Lincoln: Fatalist, Skeptic, Atheist, or Christian?* (1942); *The Religion of Abraham Lincoln* (1963); *Abraham Lincoln, Theologian of American Anguish* (1973); and *Lincoln's Greatest Speech* (2002). The last book, by Ronald C. White, dean and professor of religious history at San Francisco State University, offers a religious exegesis of Lincoln's Second Inaugural Address.

†Unlike *The Age of Reason*, Volney's book, a rambling meditation on his travels in the Levantine Empire, has not stood the test of time. His excoriation of dictatorship, coupled with flowery conversations with ghosts and reflections on ruins, seems almost unreadable today, but it was extremely popular among freethinkers in both the United States and Europe through the mid-nineteenth century.

demands that he call on divine authority as a justification
for political decisions. The most explicit of these came in
1862, when Lincoln responded sardonically to a proposal
from a mass assembly of Chicago Protestants that he issue
a proclamation immediately emancipating slaves:

> I am approached with the most opposite opinions and
> advice, and that by religious men, who are equally
> certain that I represent the Divine will. I am sure that
> either the one or the other is mistaken in that belief,
> and perhaps in some respects both. I hope it will not
> be irreverent for me to say that if it is probable that
> God would reveal his will to others, on a point so
> connected with my duty, it might be supposed that
> he would reveal it directly to me; for unless I am more
> deceived in myself than I often am, it is my earnest
> desire to know the will of Providence in this matter.
> *And if I can learn what it is, I will do it!* These are not,
> however, the days of miracles, and I suppose it will be
> granted that I am not to expect a direct revelation. I
> must study the plain, physical facts of the case, ascer-
> tain what is possible, and learn what appears to be
> wise and right.[6]

It is unsurprising that Ingersoll would find a warmer reception in the party founded on the memory of a martyred president who had explicitly rejected divine reve-

lation as a policy justification than he would in the Democratic Party, which, by the end of the century, would choose as its standard-bearer the champion of revealed religion William Jennings Bryan. Ulysses S. Grant, who succeeded Andrew Johnson as president, was another Republican who not only refused to join a church but also suggested that it might be a good idea to eliminate property tax exemptions for religious institutions.

Grant's proposal that churches pay taxes went nowhere, but Republican efforts to bar any tax support for religious schools were more successful during Grant's two-term presidency. In 1875, as Speaker of the House, Blaine nearly succeeded in persuading Congress to pass a constitutional amendment—first suggested by James Madison during the debate over ratification of the Bill of Rights and recently proposed by President Grant—that would in effect have extended the First Amendment's establishment clause to the states. The Blaine amendment stipulated that "no state shall make any law respecting an establishment of religion, or prohibiting the free exercise thereof; and no money raised by school taxation in any State, for the support of public schools, or derived from any public fund thereto, shall ever be raised under the control of any religious sect; nor shall any money so raised, or lands so devoted, be divided between religious sects or denominations." The amendment passed the House 180 to 7 and fell just four votes short in the Senate of receiving the two-thirds majority required for presentation to the states for ratification. Sixteen states soon passed their own constitutional amendments forbidding aid to religious schools (they too were popularly known as Blaine amendments), and more than half of the fifty states now have similar laws that stand as a powerful barrier to the efforts of many religions to obtain taxpayer support, by the back door if not the front, for their schools.

Ingersoll himself was strongly opposed to public funding of any and all religious education, but there is little doubt that Blaine and much of the Republican WASP establishment was motivated as much by anti-Catholicism as by Madisonian constitutional principles. The Catholic Church—which benefited so much in the United States from the absence of a state-established religion—nevertheless wanted tax money for its schools. There was no federal aid to education of any kind at the time, so the political battle over tax support for religious education was fought solely at the state level. Protestants were still (though not for long) in charge of most big-city governments, and the old-line WASPs saw Catholic schools in particular as a threat to the assimilation of growing numbers of immigrants. Ingersoll supported the Blaine amendments not because he had a special animus toward Catholicism (although he considered the recently asserted doctrine of papal infallibility even more ridiculous than most religious teachings) but because Catholicism was the only religion attempting to establish a large school system as an alternative to public education and lobbying for public funding. When Blaine finally won the Republican nomination in 1884, he did everything possible to distance himself from Ingersoll and his antireligious views, which were much more widely known than they had been in 1876.

As events unfolded, Blaine might have been better advised to distance himself from his orthodox supporters among the Protestant clergy. He lost the election because he lost New York State and is generally thought to have done so because one of his prominent Presbyterian backers, the Reverend Samuel D. Buchard, described the Democrats as the party of "rum, Romanism, and rebellion." Blaine had attended the speech, refused to disavow the remarks, and lost the state by only one thousand votes—a margin that might well have been provided by angry Irish Catholic voters in New York City. Ingersoll told reporters that he stayed out of the fray because he did not want to add fuel to the fire with his reputation as one who disdained all religion. In a letter to his brother-in-law and publisher Clint Farrell, he wrote that he pitied the six hundred Protestant ministers who had promised

Blaine "the support of Jehovah and Co.—I hate to have the old firm disappointed."[7] He also told reporters that one of the causes of Blaine's defeat had been his earlier campaign statement that "the State cannot get along without the Church" (which would seem to directly contradict the Republican candidate's early opposition to tax support for parochial schools).[8] Ingersoll commented, "If I had been in politics at the time, I would have called a meeting that night to denounce him [Blaine], even though I had made fifty speeches before supporting him."[9]

With the exception of the Blaine contretemps, Ingersoll's political oratory on behalf of Republican candidates rarely focused on church-state issues. Yet the press, especially newspapers affiliated with the Democratic Party, frequently used Ingersoll's involvement in Republican politics to attack the party of Lincoln. "The party which employs such agents to sustain its falling vitality had better die a quiet death," the *New York Sun* commented after Ingersoll's endorsement of Blaine in 1876. "To give him praise, to circulate his worthless wit, is an outrage. The only office which the press ought to perform is to help exterminate such a moral pestilence or hang the mortal carrion in chains upon a cross beam."[10] Such reactions deterred future Republican presidents from appointing Ingersoll to any office that required Senate confirmation—

even if they had sought his oratorical support before being elected.

Nevertheless, there is little question that Ingersoll's prominence in politics and in the courtroom won a broad audience for his skeptical religious views that he would not otherwise have attracted. Freethinkers had widely varying politics, and Ingersoll's Republican credentials were of little importance to them (especially since many of his positions, such as lifelong support for women's rights, were unpopular among the men who ran both parties). But there is no question that Ingersoll's reputation as a political and a courtroom orator piqued the interest of Americans who were *not* freethinkers, agnostics, or atheists but were interested in being entertained by a witty talker. Harry Thurston Peck, a stuffy and religiously orthodox classics scholar at Columbia University, may well have been right when he argued, after Ingersoll's death, that the Great Agnostic would probably have been ignored by respectable God-fearing folk if he had originally appeared on the national stage as a militant advocate of freethought rather than as a political orator. "Had he in the first place sought for widespread recognition as an opponent of Christianity, and of revealed religion, he would no doubt have gathered audiences; yet they would not have been precisely the same kind of audiences. . . . Hence it came about that instead of declaiming to the sort of audiences that usually gather to applaud the wonted peripatetic infidel—a crowd of illiterate or half-educated men, of long-haired agitators and obscene fanatics—Colonel Ingersoll delivered his attacks on Christianity before audiences made up in part, at least, of intelligent, serious-minded men and women. The political partisan had won a hearing for the professional atheist."[11] Peck did not, of course, intend this observation as a compliment to the Great Agnostic; on the contrary, he considered Ingersoll's political and legal career a Trojan horse for his true vocation as an eviscerator of religion. In his reference to "long-haired agitators and obscene fanatics," Peck was returning to a theme that first surfaced in the United States after the French Revolution, when the defenders of religious orthodoxy launched an attack on the secular Enlightenment ideals that played such an important role in the political philosophy of the founding generation. With their castigation of Thomas Paine in the closing years of the eighteenth century and the first decade of the nineteenth century, religious reactionaries attempted to equate the separation of church and state with the violent Jacobin period of the French Revolution.

By the end of the Gilded Age, which coincided with Ingersoll's death, both the champions of evangelical fundamentalism and the defenders of conventional WASP civil religion (Peck belonged in the latter category) were beginning to link the freethought movement with anarchism, socialism, Bolshevism, and immigration—especially Jewish immigration. In the years between the end of the Civil War and the beginning of the First World War, the leaders of American freethought were almost entirely homegrown. There were few personal ties between the most prominent American freethinkers and the vibrant, education-hungry Jewish immigrant culture. Nevertheless, the Yiddish translations of Ingersoll's works indicate that there was an audience among working-class Jewish readers, especially second-generation immigrants, for a skeptical view of religion that included Judaism itself. Furthermore, the new immigrants from Russia and eastern Europe (like the earlier generation of German Jewish immigrants) strongly supported the freethought position on the separation of church and state. Just as strongly, they opposed tax support for religious schools—for the obvious reason that only in America, with its nonsectarian tax-supported schools, were Jews able to satisfy the hunger for education that had been frustrated throughout the Tsarist empire.

These new Americans almost certainly were not the people Peck had in mind when he talked about the "intelligent, serious-minded men and women" who continued to display a regrettable interest in Ingersoll's speeches. Peck was, no doubt, referring to Republican businessmen who stood outside Ingersoll's lecture venues in New York for hours in hopes of obtaining a ticket, only to find that no one was willing to sell to scalpers at any price. He was referring to an eminently respectable audience in 1880 at Booth's Theater on East Twenty-Third Street in Manhattan, where, the *New York Times* reported disapprovingly, the audience consisted "half of ladies."[12] Or perhaps Peck was thinking of Mrs. Anna M. Brooks, a Texas rancher's wife who, in 1896, rode more than thirty miles on horseback to hear Ingersoll's "The Liberty of Man, Woman, and Child" in the town of Sherman (pop. circa 9,000). When Mrs. Brooks rode into town, she headed straight for Sherman's best hotel, where she was sure that the Great Agnostic would be staying. In the dining room, she introduced herself to Eva Ingersoll, who invited her up to her room to meet her husband. "We shook hands," Mrs. Brooks reported in a letter to the national freethought publication the *Truth Seeker*; "and when I told him how far I rode through the mud to see him and hear him he said he would give me a pass to the lecture. I thanked him but told him I thought myself fortunate that I had already bought my seat in a good place. He said he was sorry I had been in such a hurry to pay out my money. . . . I gave Mrs. Ingersoll my recipe for biscuit."[13]

In any case, it was difficult to portray a freethinker who reached out to audiences throughout the nation, and whose fans included ranchers' wives bearing biscuit recipes, as an alien in thrall to threatening European philosophies. As the young historian Sidney Warren observed in 1943, "Ingersoll was as much a part of his native land as Bunker Hill, as the Declaration of Independence and Abraham Lincoln. He knew and liked his America, but unlike another fighting Bob—LaFollette of Wisconsin, who spent his time combatting the practical evils of modern society—Ingersoll devoted his efforts to long-range objectives, divorced from immediate economic and social issues. None of his efforts could possibly have been crowned with immediate success; hence the road which Ingersoll traveled was less likely to bring him current recognition and fame. But Ingersoll was satisfied that he was dealing with the fundamental principles of society, and that his labors were of basic importance."[14]

Perhaps no episode in Ingersoll's career provides such a telling example of the melding of broad and elevated cultural aspirations with deeply American roots as the dedication speech he delivered on January 25, 1893, at a theater in Dowagiac, Michigan. The new theater and opera house was named in memory of the town's leading freethinker and employer, the felicitously named Philo D. Beckwith. On that night, workers from Beckwith's Round Oak Company, one of the largest manufacturers of stoves and furnaces in the last quarter of the nineteenth century, joined a crowd of nationally recognized artists, business leaders, and philanthropists who had traveled to the small town in southwestern Michigan for the dedication.

Beckwith was a paternalistic employer whose high wages and benefits, including the then-rare concession of sick pay, had protected Dowagiac from the increasingly violent labor clashes taking place in urban America throughout the 1880s—including, most notably, the bloody Haymarket Square affair in nearby Chicago in 1886, when an explosion of unknown origin prompted police to fire into a crowd demonstrating peacefully on behalf of an eight-hour workday, and seven officers, along with many more demonstrators, wound up dead. In his hometown, Beckwith attempted to promote freethought through educational programs designed to expose local residents to the ideas of those he considered the heroes of the human race. The theater dedicated by Ingersoll featured a wide variety of Beckwith's favorite freethinkers, writers, and artists in busts on the facade. Among the figures, carved in Lake Superior red sandstone, were Ingersoll, Paine, Voltaire, Susan B. Anthony, George Eliot, Victor Hugo, George Sand, Walt Whitman, Goethe, Shakespeare, Beethoven, and Chopin. Ingersoll, speaking to the heterogeneous audience before him, described the theater as a "fitting monument to the man whose memory we honor—to one who, broadening with the years, outgrew the cruel creeds, the heartless dogmas of his time—from religion to reason—from theology to humanity—from slavery to freedom—from the shadow of fear to the blessed light of love and courage." Describing Beckwith as one "who believed in intellectual hospitality—in the perfect freedom of the heart and soul," Ingersoll went on to pay homage to the men and women portrayed on the building's facade as exemplars of the achievements most prized by freethinkers. It was fitting, he said, that the monument to Beckwith should "be adorned with the sublime faces, wrought in stone, of the immortal dead—of those who battled for the rights of man—who broke the fetters of the slave—of those who filled the minds of men with poetry, art, and light." Ingersoll praised Voltaire, "who abolished torture in France," and Paine, "whose pen did as much as any sword to make the New World free." Many of the writers most deeply admired by Ingersoll were honored on the facade—including Victor Hugo, "who wept for those who weep"; Walt Whitman, "author of the tenderest, the most pathetic, the sublimest poem that this continent has produced"; George Eliot, "who wove within her brain the purple robe her genius wears"; and "Shakespeare; the King of all."[15]

The Beckwith Memorial Theater was a true Gilded Age monument to the broad cultural scope of the American freethought movement. What distinguished the pantheon was its combination of Americans and foreigners; men and women; political thinkers, agnostics, and artists; the honored dead and the controversial living—the last group including Ingersoll himself. The heretical and lusty poems of Whitman, who had died in 1892, were still considered scandalous trash by much of the reading public and by orthodox literary critics. Ingersoll, in an 1892 eulogy for Whitman reprinted around the country, had predicted that the poet "will be understood yet, and that for which he was condemned—his frankness, his candor—will add to the glory and greatness of his fame" (see Appendix A).[16] Both Ingersoll and the Beckwith Theater represented not a majority of Americans but one important strand in the cultural fabric of a period in which many citizens, ranging from freethinking ranchers to civic leaders, valued intellectual curiosity more than they feared the unknown consequences of free inquiry.

On the eve of the dedication speech, the local newspaper perfectly captured the combination of ambivalence and respect with which Ingersoll was viewed by his contemporaries. In a burst of boosterish hyperbole, the *Dowagiac Times* expressed delight at the prospect of listening to "the greatest reasoner, advocate, poet and orator the world has ever known and all at home." The paper took care to point out that "few among us agree with him in politics, religion, and all minor points" but that "every good man and woman agrees in the supreme right to disagree. We would not wish to live in a world where honest discussion was a lost art."[17] There was no chance of that with Bob Ingersoll coming to town.

III

Champion of Science

The church still faithfully guards the dangerous tree of
knowledge, and has exerted in all ages her utmost power
to keep mankind from eating the fruit thereof.
—RGI, "The Gods"

The primary secular argument against the validity of religious belief, whether advanced in philosophical or scientific terms, has always been grounded in the premise
that knowledge based on observation of the natural world,
however faulty or incomplete initial conclusions may
prove upon further observation, is inherently superior to
faith based on mythic events that contradict the verifiable
laws of nature. This was as true in the eighteenth century
as in the nineteenth, but Robert Ingersoll's generation had
an inestimable advantage over the religious heretics of
the Enlightenment. By the second half of the nineteenth
century, freethinkers could point to the technological
fruits of once-theoretical science as evidence of progress

that greatly benefited the human species in ways that ordinary people could see and understand. All of Ingersoll's lectures were infused with the conviction that scientists and inventors had done much more for the welfare of human beings than preachers of any creed. On the frontispiece of the first edition of his collected works, a blasphemous cartoon embodies this theme. In one row of Latin crosses, marked with the slogan "FOR THE LOVE OF GOD," people are being put to death; in another row, labeled "FOR THE USE OF MAN," the crosses are actually telephone polls connected by wires.

Unlike the telephone, many nineteenth-century technological advances contradicted the injunctions of writings once—and quite recently in a historical sense—held sacred by nearly all. "In sorrow thou shalt bring forth children," the Lord told the disobedient Eve—but ether and chloroform were being used to ease the suffering of women in childbirth in all of the world's most advanced nations. Fiery preachers might still say that it violated God's plan for women to be freed from the promised anguish attached to childbearing, just as many of their clerical predecessors had said, at the beginning of the century, that vaccination against smallpox usurped the divine prerogative—but few people were listening if they had the means to pay a doctor skilled in the use of the effective new painkillers. Of even greater importance than contradictions between a literal reading of scripture and the use of specific medical advances like anesthesia was the general advance in understanding of the natural world. The idea that infectious diseases were caused by invisible organisms called bacteria, for example, was originally considered as dubious and unproven as Darwin's theory of evolution. From the 1860s through the 1890s, however, the pioneering research and experiments of Louis Pasteur in France and bacteriologist Robert Koch in Germany began to be widely known among educated specialists around the world, including the United States. Leading American surgeons began to use aseptic routines, pioneered by England's Joseph Lister, and even the more progressive general practitioners, in cities and rural areas, came to realize that they could prevent many common diseases simply by washing their hands and keeping themselves and their patients as clean as possible. As understanding of the natural causes of fatal illnesses grew, supernatural explanations for certain kinds of human suffering became unnecessary. This was the fertile environment in which Ingersoll preached the gospel of science as the major source of human progress and religious superstition as its enemy—a force through which "the heart hardens and the brain softens." To those who insisted that superstition, whether channeled through folk tales or formal religious institutions, was harmless, Ingersoll replied that belief in the supernatural wastes human energies by diverting them into the search for a nonexistent, miraculous protection. "Credulity, ceremony, worship, sacrifice and prayer take the place of honest work, of investigation, of intellectual effort, of observation, of experience. Progress becomes impossible."[1]

While it was difficult for any cleric other than an unreconstructed Calvinist (and strict Calvinism had, after all, been losing ground in America since the end of the seventeenth century) to convince the public that new drugs to ease pain were ungodly, Darwin's theory of evolution was another matter altogether. Evolution did—as it still does—pose a direct challenge not only to the creation story of Genesis but, for many, to the basic belief that man is a being created by God in the divine image. And evolution—unlike, say, the discovery of the role of bacteria in transmitting disease—had no immediate, easily understandable practical benefits to offer the human species. Moreover, there could be no visible scientific demonstrations—unlike, say, Pasteur's famous experiments in the 1860s and 1870s that produced a safer milk supply and a method of inoculation to protect sheep from anthrax—to prove that humans were descended from lower animals. Backward-looking clerics like the Reverend Thomas A. Eliot could simply dismiss fossils offered as evidence to support Darwin's theory by pointing out that no living human had ever actually seen one animal turning into another.*

In 1876, when Ingersoll was beginning his career as a national speaker, Thomas Henry Huxley visited the United States for the first time. He delivered three lectures about evolution to standing-room-only audiences in New York City, and, although his speeches were described thoroughly and fairly in the news columns, the editorial pages of the *New York Times* reflected the profound unease aroused by Darwin's theory among well-educated business leaders, scholars, and politicians, many of whom were no more willing than their poorer, less educated contemporaries to abandon their view of themselves as special, divinely infused beings. The *Times's* editorial writers, having heard Huxley's argument, insisted that the theory of evolution by means of natural selection not only should but must be modified by scientists so that it posed no challenge to belief in a divine creator. This was possible, the editorial suggested, because geological discoveries indicating that the earth was older than the time frame in Genesis had in fact demonstrated "a striking general coincidence between the Mosaic narrative and modern

---

*This argument can still be found in unsophisticated fundamentalist antievolution literature and on anti-evolution Web sites, although it is not as common as it was a century ago. Even the most obdurate anti-evolutionists today are well aware that the emergence of new species, including *Homo sapiens*, took place over a period of time that could never have been witnessed by one man from beginning to end.

geological theories. And Biblical scholars have changed many of our former interpretations of these records."[2] The obvious hole in the argument is that the biblical scholars, not the geologists, were the ones who had modified their views in a tortuous effort to prove that there was no real contradiction between the story of Genesis and contemporary geological conclusions. Huxley had compared Darwin's theory to Copernicus's heliocentric theory of the solar system, but the *Times* dismissed the analogy as evidence of "how far [astray] theory will lead a clear brain."[3]

In this anxious intellectual climate, with new scientific concepts impinging on humanity's cherished sense of itself as the summa of creation, Ingersoll began speaking out on behalf of Darwin's theory. The scientific basis of the theory was understood by only a tiny proportion of highly educated Americans, but the potential threat to religious faith was perceived even by those who did not understand the science. Ingersoll's contribution to the debate was to speak directly to the wounded self-image of those who believed that if humans were deprived of their divine provenance, they were therefore nothing—that a creature descended from beings who had struggled out of a primal ooze could not possibly consider himself only a little lower than the angels. "I believe that man came up from lower animals," Ingersoll declared in 1877, only six years after Darwin, in *The Descent of Man*, had directly addressed the religion-shattering implications of the general theory he had outlined in *On the Origin of Species* in 1859. "When I first heard of that doctrine I did not like it," Ingersoll acknowledged, adding that he became convinced of the validity of evolutionary thought only after careful reading. Then Ingersoll straightforwardly addressed the fear that any admission of descent from lesser animals nullified the achievements of human beings:

After all I had rather belong to a race that started from the skull-less vertebrates in the dim Laurentian seas, vertebrates wiggling without knowing why they wiggled, swimming without knowing where they were going, but that in some way began to develop, and began to get a little higher and a little higher in the scale of existence; that they came up by degrees through millions of ages through all the animal world, though all that crawls and swims and floats and climbs and creeps, and finally produced the gentleman in the dug-out; and then from this man, getting a little grander, and each one calling every one who made a little advance an infidel or an atheist—for in the history of this world the man who is ahead has always been called a heretic—I would rather come from a race that started from that skull-less vertebrate, and came up and up and up and finally produced Shakespeare, the man who found the human intellect dwelling in a hut, touched it with the wand of his genius and it became a palace domed and pinnacled. . . . I would rather belong to that race that commenced a skull-less vertebrate and produced Shakespeare, a race that has before it an infinite future, with an angel of progress leaning from the far horizon, beckoning men forward, upward and onward forever—I had rather belong to such a race, commencing there, producing this, and with that hope, than to have sprung from a perfect pair upon which the Lord has lost money every moment from that day to this.[4]

Ingersoll's message had a special resonance precisely because he admitted to having sustained an initial shock at the idea that instead of being the great singular creature who commands all lower beings in the divinely ordained hierarchy of nature, a human being was only a part of nature. What Ingersoll told his audiences was that they too could get over the short-lived trauma of the loss of human exceptionalism—that being a part of nature, if one was a man or woman of reason, provided not only a sufficient but an excellent reason to live. This optimistic message, well suited to Americans, whose most distinctive national trait was their belief in progress, was that the human species is even more remarkable if descended from beings who emerged from more primitive organisms. *Look at how far we have come, not where we came from,* Ingersoll told his fellow Americans. *Look forward to what we may become.* His optimism directly contradicted the despairing fatalism of the orthodox clergymen who preached that man would lose all dignity if evolution were ever to be widely accepted. This point of view was well expressed in an "Apostate's Creed," written by an anonymous author and published in a major Christian periodical. If the evolutionists triumphed, the author predicted, a new creed would have to read: "I believe in the wholly impersonal absolute, the wholly uncatholic church, the disunion of saints, the survival of the fittest, the persistency of force, the dispersion of the body, and in death everlasting."[5] Nonsense, said Ingersoll, declaring cheerfully and blasphemously, "Religion has not civilized man—man has civilized religion. God improves as man advances."

Furthermore, acceptance of the natural origins and evolution of man was integrally linked with the effort to alleviate suffering long attributed to supernatural causes. "The moment it is admitted that all phenomena are within the domain of the natural, the necessity for a priest has disappeared," Ingersoll argued. "Religion breathes the air of the supernatural. . . . As long as plagues and pestilences could be stopped by prayer, the priest was useful. The moment the physician found a cure, the priest became an extravagance."[6] That science had not yet found ways to effectively treat, much less cure, diseases like cancer did not render them supernatural mysteries but simply meant that human understanding of nature was incomplete.

One of Ingersoll's most valuable contributions to the emerging, enlivened dialogue between representatives of science and religion was his refusal to take refuge, as liberal Protestant clerics did, in the conviction that only strict biblical literalism posed a formidable barrier to the reconciliation of religion and faith. Ingersoll gave no more credence to William Paley's argument that the existence of a watch implied the existence of an infallible watchmaker—the forerunner of today's "intelligent design" argument—than he did to the story of the six days of creation in Genesis. Like most agnostics and atheists before and after him, Ingersoll went straight to the theodicy problem to refute design—intelligent or unintelligent.

In "The Gods," a speech he began delivering in the early 1870s, before he was a nationally known orator, Ingersoll mocked the tendency of religious believers to attribute everything good and beautiful in the world to a divine creator and everything evil to either the devil or a mysterious divine plan that passeth all understanding. "Did it ever occur to them that a cancer is as beautiful in its development as the reddest rose?" he asked—a question that frequently shocked even the nonbelievers in his audiences. "How beautiful the process of digestion! By what ingenious methods the blood is poisoned so that the cancer shall have food! By what wonderful contrivances the entire system of man is made to pay tribute to this divine and charming cancer! . . . See how it gradually but surely expands and grows! By what marvelous mechanism it is supplied with long and slender roots that reach out to the most secret nerves of pain for sustenance and life! . . . Seen through the microscope it is a miracle of order and beauty. . . . Think of the amount of thought it must have required to invent a way by which the life of one man might be given to produce one cancer? Is it possible to look upon it and doubt that there is design in the universe, and that the inventor of this wonderful cancer must be infinitely powerful, ingenious and good?"[7]

To the oft-repeated orthodox religious argument that the theory of evolution degraded man, Ingersoll responded that precisely the opposite was the case. "The church teaches that man was created perfect and that for six thousand years he has degenerated," he observed. "Darwin demonstrated the falsity of this dogma. He shows that man has for thousands of ages steadily advanced; that the Garden of Eden is an ignorant myth; that the doctrine of original sin has no foundation in fact; that the atonement is an absurdity; that the serpent did not tempt, and that man did not 'fall.'"[8]

What made Ingersoll more effective as a communicator of science and reason than intellectuals of great distinction like Huxley was his capacity to explain—but not oversimplify—complex subjects for Americans who might have no more than a few years of formal education. In 1911, Ingersoll's near-contemporary Herman Kittredge described the orator as "preeminently the teacher of the masses. Farmers, mechanics, laborers, used to say, on hearing his explanation . . . 'Well, I can understand that *now*.'"[9] In describing the impact of an orator who lived and died before the age of sound recording, one can only rely on the descriptions of his contemporaries. One of the most precise accounts of Ingersoll's success at communicating with ordinary people appears in a volume by Hamlin Garland, who noted that Ingersoll strode briskly onto the stage and began to speak almost before he left the wings—as if he simply could not wait to share his thoughts with the audience. "He appeared to be speaking to each one of us individually," Garland recalled. "His tone was confidential, friendly, and yet authoritative. 'Do you know,' he began, 'that every race has created all its gods and all its devils? The childhood of the race put faries in the breeze and a kobold in every stream." Garland described

Ingersoll's effect on the audience in much the same way that the Chicago newspapers had described the "Plumed Knight" speech in 1876. "He bantered us, challenged us, electrified us. At times his eloquence held us silent as images and then some witty turn, some humorous phrase, brought roars of applause. At times we cheered almost every sentence like delegates at a political convention. At other moments we rose in our seats and yelled. There was something hypnotic in his rhythm as well as in his marvelous lines like a Saxon minstrel. . . . He taught me the value of speaking as if thinking out loud. After hearing him, the harsh, monotonous cadences of other orators became a weariness."[10]

In his speeches about religion (in contrast to his earlier, more florid political speeches), Ingersoll avoided the flights of hyperbole characteristic of many orators of his era. William Jennings Bryan's famous "cross of gold" speech, accepting the Democratic presidential nomination in 1896, was the antithesis of Ingersoll's style.* Ingersoll's tone was informal, his language colloquial, and his humor dry and direct. "It is this quality which made his 'Mistakes of Moses' irresistible even to his opponents," Garland remembered. "I recall his roguish look when after he had

---

*The best-known line in this speech is, "You shall not press down upon the brow of labor this crown of thorns. You shall not crucify mankind upon a cross of gold."

computed that in order to produce a flood which would cover the tops of the mountains in the space of forty days and forty nights, it would be necessary to have something like ten feet of rain per hour, he suddenly asked, 'How is that for dampness?' He was not merely humorous; he was witty. He had an Irishman's ability to answer on the spot."[11]

Ingersoll's emphasis on logic appealed not only, or even predominantly, to those prepared to reject religion altogether but to those who wished to reconcile their religion with science. Unlike some of the most prominent figures among the "new atheists" today, Ingersoll was more than willing to find common ground, when that was possible, with reform-minded religious leaders like his close personal friend Henry Ward Beecher and Felix Adler, the Reform Jew who founded the Society for Ethical Culture. Ingersoll played a particularly important role in the widening of the division between mainstream American Protestantism and right-wing evangelical fundamentalism—a far-reaching schism that continues to this day and has contributed mightily to the culture wars that have infused American politics and religion since the 1980s.

Yet Ingersoll could also be as acerbic as Richard Dawkins and Sam Harris about what he considered the irreconcilability of religion and science. Nothing that the "new atheists" have written could be any more offensive to devout believers than Ingersoll's observation, in 1885, that religion had sought to strangle science in its cradle. "Now that science has attained its youth," Ingersoll said, "and superstition is in its dotage, the trembling, palsied wreck says to the athlete: 'Let us be friends.' It reminds me of the bargain the cock wished to make with the horse: 'Let us agree not to step on each other's feet.'"[12] Nevertheless, Ingersoll's rejection of all religion as superstition did not prevent him from recognizing that any move away from biblical literalism on the part of religion was good for freethought. "Mr. Beecher is trying to do something to harmonize superstition and science," Ingersoll told *Truth Seeker.* "He is reading between the lines. He has discovered that Darwin is only a later Saint Paul, or that Saint Paul was the original Darwin. He is endeavoring to make the New Testament a scientific text-book. Of course he will fail. But his intentions are good. Thousands of people will read the New Testament with more freedom than heretofore. They will look for new meanings; and he who looks for new meanings will not be satisfied with the old ones."[13] In reading this passage, one is struck by the capacity of at least some prominent nineteenth-century public antagonists to disagree sharply and remain on not only civil but cordial terms. Beecher was a frequent guest at Ingersoll's parties at his home in Gramercy

Park, which also included some of the most famous musicians, actors, writers, and public officials—of varying religious and political persuasions—on the New York scene.

Beecher once introduced Ingersoll at a political rally as a man "that for a full score and more of years has worked for the right in the great, broad field of humanity, and for the cause of human rights."* Ingersoll himself delivered a eulogy for Beecher at his funeral in 1884, and this speech reached millions who read it in liberal Protestant publications and in magazines and newspapers intended for a general audience. This tribute to the liberalizing religious impulse represented by Beecher does much to explain why Ingersoll's influence extended far beyond the relatively small circle of Americans who were proud to call themselves agnostics, atheists, or even freethinkers. As the mourners knew well, Beecher, born in 1813, was the son of the Reverend Lyman Beecher, one of the most influential and theologically retrograde American ministers of the nineteenth century. Ingersoll described his friend's childhood as a "Puritan penitentiary" that "despised every natural joy, hated pictures, abhorred statues as lewd and lustful things, execrated music, regarded nature as fallen

---

*This speech was delivered at the Brooklyn Academy of Music, and Horace Greeley's *New York Herald* described the scene in its edition of October 31, 1880: "When the expounder of the Gospel of Christ took the famous atheist by the hand, and shook it fervently, saying that he respected and honored him for the honesty of his convictions and his splendid labors for patriotism and the country . . . the great building trembled with a storm of applause."

and corrupt, man as totally depraved and woman as somewhat worse." Nevertheless, young Henry had caught glimpses of a larger world "through the grated windows of his cell. . . . Another heaven bent above his life." When Beecher became a minister, he moved away from the theory of predestined damnation that his father had taught him. In Ingersoll's view, Beecher had "passed from harsh and cruel creeds to that serene philosophy that has no place for pride or hate, that threatens no revenge, that looks on sin as stumblings of the blind and pities those who fall, knowing that in the souls of all there is a sacred yearning for life . . . that men are part of Nature's self—kindred of all life—the gradual growth of countless years; that all the sacred books were helps until outgrown, and all religions rough and devious paths that man has worn with weary feet in sad and painful search for truth and peace."[14]

Ingersoll's appreciation of Beecher as a person, and as a religious leader who had helped move his own denomination toward a god of love rather than a god of vengeance, in no way implied that the Great Agnostic himself subscribed to a diluted brand of Christianity. Rather, Ingersoll considered it a great social boon that the religion practiced by a majority of his countrymen had produced at least some preachers who wanted to forge an accommodation between faith and science. For his part, Beecher—

despite his sincere friendship with Ingersoll—did not entirely dismiss the idea that there must be some sort of reckoning in an afterlife for those who had rejected religion altogether. He once remarked, apropos of Ingersoll's well-known love of the poetry of Robert Burns, that Ingersoll's epitaph might well turn out to be "Robert burns."[15]

Ingersoll did not, of course, agree with the Protestant accommodationists who were willing to concede the validity of evolution while maintaining that God was the prime instigator of the process. Like atheists today, Ingersoll argued that no all-powerful God, as conventionally imagined by orthodox believers, would have been such a bumbler as to set in motion a process of creation that involved billions of years and the appearance and subsequent extinction of entire species. He was, however, convinced that the progress of science, and the growing acceptance of evolution—even in a limited way—by liberal Protestants would inevitably create more atheists, agnostics, and freethinkers and that science would eventually render all religious creeds obsolete. The sharp increase in just the past twenty years in the number of Americans who belong to no church and consider their outlook on public affairs predominantly secular indicates that Ingersoll was right about the connection between religious liberalism and secularism. But the persistent presence of a large proportion of hard-core biblical literalists in this country—

an oft-told story beyond the scope of this book—was not anticipated either by freethinkers or by proponents of "rational" religion at the end of the nineteenth century. There is no question, though, that the large and hetero-geneous audiences attracted to Ingersoll's lectures, and his ability to charm and lay out some areas of agreement with more progressive members of the clergy, gave rise to a new generation of Americans who were unwilling to say a flat no to science on religious grounds and who edu-cated their children in the opening decades of the twenti-eth century in religious adaptation rather than resistance to science.

Ingersoll took aim at the structure of religious belief at its weakest point—the growing realization in the late nineteenth century that if ancient afflictions long thought to be of divine origin could be eliminated through the intelligent efforts of man, the divine origins could no lon-ger be taken for granted. In 1898, when President William McKinley issued a proclamation thanking God for the American victory at Santiago de Cuba, the site of Teddy Roosevelt's charge up San Juan Hill during the Spanish-American War, Ingersoll slyly wondered why the presi-dent did not also thank God for sending the yellow fever that killed so many Spanish soldiers and seamen.

Ingersoll's deepest belief, and the reason for the seduc-tiveness of his oratory, was that the removal of one illogical chink in the edifice of supernaturalism could bring the whole structure tumbling down. Darwin's vision of human evolution, with "the most exalted object we are capable of conceiving"—higher animals—produced from "the war of nature, from famine and death" was a flaw in the very foundation of humanity's claim to a share in divinity. Fundamentalists, in Ingersoll's time as well as our own, understood this instinctively in a way that more reason-oriented religious leaders like Beecher did not. Darwin's famous concluding statement from *On the Origin of Species* was one of Ingersoll's favorite passages in the English language: "There is a grandeur in this view of life, with its several powers, having been breathed into a few forms or into one; and that, whilst this planet has gone on cycling along according to the fixed law of gravity, from so simple a beginning endless forms most beautiful and most wonderful have been, and are being, evolved." To Ingersoll, this language was more inspirational than the Bible precisely because it did not rest on a repudiation of nature in order to envisage future, higher possibilities for man as nature's most intelligent creature.

IV

The Humanistic Freethinker

While I am opposed to all orthodox creeds, I have a
creed myself; and my creed is this. Happiness is the
only good. The time to be happy is now. The place to be
happy is here. The way to be happy is to make others so.
The creed is somewhat short, but it is long enough for
this life, strong enough for this world. If there is another
world, when we get there we can make another creed.
                                        —RGI

Robert Green Ingersoll's "happiness creed," frequently
included in his speeches and recorded for posterity in
1894 in Thomas Edison's original New Jersey laboratory,
combines his antireligious views with humanistic, classi-
cally liberal social thought in ways that not only made
him difficult to pigeonhole among his freethinking contemporaries but would also render him an elusive figure
for biographers in the second half of the twentieth century.* As a Gilded Age Republican who considered the alleviation of poverty a social responsibility, an individualist

---

*A sound recording of Ingersoll reciting this creed, which he used in many
speeches, can be heard by visitors to the Ingersoll Birthplace-Museum in Dresden, New York. The recording was originally made by Ingersoll in Thomas
Edison's laboratory in New Jersey and has been remastered several times.

and libertarian who insisted that government protect the rights of minorities, an economic conservative on some issues but an advocate for social reform who often sounded like Thomas Paine and John Stuart Mill, Ingersoll held opinions that sometimes seemed contradictory even to contemporaries who deeply admired him for his opposition to religion. Thus, it is not surprising that Ingersoll has been misunderstood to some extent by many of his biographers—especially because Republicanism in the late twentieth century fused religious orthodoxy with economic conservatism.

Until the late 1890s, when President McKinley elicited Ingersoll's scorn by declaring that God had been on our side in the Spanish-American War, national Republican politicians took care to distance themselves from those who wished to claim divine sanction for political actions. Abraham Lincoln, whose political guile has been sanctified by time, evaded the demands of a powerful group of Protestant ministers who, in 1864, asked him to support a constitutional amendment establishing God in general, and Christ in particular, as the source of American governmental authority—thereby remedying the theocratically inexcusable failure of the framers to cast their eyes heavenward beyond "we the people." Lincoln promised the overwrought clerics that he would "take such action upon it as my responsibility to my Maker and our country demands."[1] In this matter, Lincoln's concept of his responsibility to both his maker and his country was to let the proposed Christian amendment die in Congress. While Lincoln's attitude toward organized religion was generally neutral, the next elected Republican president, Ulysses S. Grant, took a stance that might reasonably be described as hostile when he put forward the ill-received suggestion that religious institutions pay property taxes.

Republicans in high office were unenthusiastic about another cause espoused by organized religion—the punitive anti-obscenity laws passed by many state legislatures and Congress and named after Anthony Comstock, the fanatical anti-vice crusader who began his career by trying to clean up prostitution and pornography in, of all places, New York City. While still in his twenties, Comstock became the president of the YMCA's New York–based Society for the Suppression of Vice, which he used as a base to lobby for both federal and state laws prohibiting the distribution of "obscene" materials through the mails. In 1877, President Rutherford B. Hayes, as a personal favor to Ingersoll, dropped a federal obscenity case against William D. Bennett, publisher of the *Truth Seeker* and one of Comstock's longtime targets. Ingersoll was no defender of even the relatively non-explicit pornographic images of his era, but he did not think the government had any business defining obscenity and was especially appalled by the Comstock Laws' classification of advertisements for or articles about contraception as obscene material (notwithstanding the inefficacy of contemporary birth control devices). Freethought newspapers did mention contraception, and the laws provided a pretext for the late nineteenth-century religious right to interfere with publications largely devoted to challenging religion and upholding the separation of church and state.* Even though Ingersoll could not run for public office and tar his party with the infernal whiff of public ungodliness, there was no reason why he could not be both an influential Republican and a freethinker. He was able to use his political clout behind the scenes with officeholders like Hayes, who had benefited from his oratory on the party's behalf. For evangelical fundamentalist Protestants like William Jennings Bryan, there was no place to go in the late nineteenth century but the Democratic Party, and the alignment lasted until the 1960s, when Democrats spearheaded passage of civil rights laws. Nineteenth-century Catholics were also overwhelmingly Democratic, not only because the Republicans rejected tax support for pa-

---

*Soap manufacturer Samuel Colgate, a major financial backer of the Society for the Suppression of Vice when it was headed by Comstock, had to withdraw an advertising campaign for his new product Vaseline when the *Truth Seeker* gleefully reprinted the company's claims that petroleum jelly was a useful method of birth control. Unfortunately, the false belief that Vaseline was an effective contraceptive lingered well into the twentieth century and was responsible for a good many unwanted pregnancies.

rochial schools but because the vast majority of Catholic immigrants were blue-collar workers whose economic interests were directly opposed to the party of the robber barons.

To a man like Bryan, who was an economic populist as well as a devout fundamentalist, Ingersoll's ties to Republican business interests were as odious as his religious iconoclasm.* As a lawyer, Ingersoll did not represent only widows and those accused of blasphemy (although he did do plenty of what would be called pro bono work today) but also politicians and government officials accused of corruption. Among the most famous of his cases were the "Star Route" trials in the early 1880s. Ingersoll, who had moved to Washington after his "Plumed Knight" speech in 1876, was lead counsel for Senator Stephen W. Dorsey, an old friend and one of the many Republicans, dating back to Grant's administration, accused of corruption in awarding postal contracts in the West. The rural postal routes, served by stagecoach and horses in parts of the nation not reachable by boat or railroads, were awarded to private businesses, and the contracts required delivery

---

*The term "fundamentalist" in its current sense, meaning one who accepts all biblical descriptions as literally true, did not enter the American language until the second decade of the twentieth century, after publication by the Bible Institute of Los Angeles of a multivolume work, *The Fundamentals*, defending orthodox Protestantism. Bryan was, however, a fundamentalist in the sense that the classification is used today.

of the mail with "certainty, celerity, and security." Since legal documents were written by hand before the typewriter became a standard office tool, tired scribes often substituted asterisks for the three nouns—hence the term "Star Route." After two lengthy trials, all of the Star Route defendants were eventually acquitted. There was little direct evidence of money actually changing hands in return for postal contracts (although there is no doubt that it happened), and juries were as skeptical about conspiracy cases in the nineteenth century as they are today. Ingersoll, because of his reputation as an antireligious orator and a spellbinder in the presence of juries, received more attention than any of the dozens of other lawyers involved in the trials. He compared Dorsey's wife, who, unusually for that time, was present in the courtroom to watch her husband's legal ordeal, to a weeping Mary Magdalene—a rhetorical flourish that goaded the government prosecutor into questioning the propriety of the Great Agnostic's allusion to a crucifixion whose redemptive value he did not acknowledge.

Ingersoll's Republican connections drew criticism even from his contemporary admirers among freethinkers on the political left. Clarence Darrow, who paid a moving tribute to the Great Agnostic shortly after Ingersoll's death in 1899, did not hesitate to speak ill of the dead only a year later. He told an audience in Chicago that although the Great Agnostic had viewed religion with unflinching rationality, he had abandoned reason on purely political issues. "The older and more venerable a political superstition," Darrow said, "the more he [Ingersoll] would cling to it."[2] Darrow was speaking primarily about Ingersoll's conservatism on economic issues like the gold standard, while ignoring Ingersoll's frequent rejections of the Gilded Age Republican party line when it conflicted with his social values. Ingersoll disagreed openly with many Republican policies, most notably the party's abandonment of civil rights in the 1880s and its hard anti-labor stance. In 1886, he supported Henry George, the author of the highly influential work *Progress and Poverty* (1879), in his unsuccessful candidacy for mayor of New York on a platform of a "single tax" on land. It is hard to imagine that a dedicated plutocrat would have believed, along with Ingersoll, that no one should be allowed to own any land he did not use personally. "And why?" Ingersoll asked. "Don't you know that if people could bottle the air, they would? Don't you know that there would be an American Air-bottling Association? And don't you know that they would allow thousands and millions to die for want of breath, if they could not pay for air?"[3] No supporter of a pure, unregulated market could have written the following passage from "Eight Hours Must Come," an essay published in 1890.

For thousands of years men have been talking and
writing about the great law of supply and demand—
and insisting that in some way this mysterious law
has governed and will continue to govern the activi-
ties of the human race. It is admitted that this law is
merciless—that when the demand fails, the producer,
the laborer, must suffer, must perish—that the law
feels neither pity nor malice—it simply acts, regardless of consequences. Under this law, capital will
employ the cheapest [means possible]. . . . The great
law has nothing to do with food or clothes, with filth
or crime. It cares nothing for homes, for peniten-
tiaries, or asylums. It simply acts—and some men
triumph, some succeed, some fail, and some perish.[4]

In this essay, Ingersoll repudiated the social Darwinism
that was as much an article of faith for many wealthy mis-
interpreters of Darwin's theory of evolution as Genesis
was for religious fundamentalists. Endorsing both the
eight-hour day and the right of workers to strike if hu-
mane working conditions could be achieved in no other
way, Ingersoll argued, "The working people should be
protected by law. If they are not, the capitalists will require just as many hours as human nature can bear. We
have seen here in America street-car drivers working sixteen and seventeen hours a day. It was necessary to have a

strike in order to get to fourteen, another strike to get to twelve, and nobody could blame them for keeping on striking till they get to eight hours."*

Ingersoll also saw a connection between secular public education and the unwillingness of workers to simply accept conditions set by their employers. Not long ago, he said, there were "no teachers except the church, and the church taught obedience and faith—told the poor people that although they had a hard time here, working for nothing, they would be paid in Paradise with a large interest." But a reward in the afterlife would no longer satisfy workers who could read, write, and think for themselves. Ingersoll made an even more extraordinary statement, coming as it did from a rich white man of his time. Economic justice, he said, must apply to women as well as to men, and working men should remember that "all who labor are their brothers, and that all women who labor are their sisters." The worst-paid, worst-treated workers in America were women, Ingersoll noted more than two decades before the Triangle Shirtwaist fire.† "Think of the sewing women in this city," he wrote, "and yet we call ourselves civilized!"[5]

---

*It should be noted that Ingersoll was using the word "capitalists" in purely descriptive fashion—meaning people who possessed capital—and neither in the pejorative way that has long been associated with far left politics or in the positive way that it is used by right-wing proponents of an unregulated market today.

†The 1911 fire, in which 145 garment workers died, remains the single deadliest workplace accident in New York City history.

This passage exemplifies the cast of mind that distinguished Ingersoll from the social Darwinists among his contemporaries—including Herbert Spencer and Yale University political scientist William Graham Sumner—who insisted that Darwin's description of "tooth-and-claw" natural selection did and should also apply to man in a state of nature. Darwin explicitly rejected this concept if applied to civilized humans. The difference between civilization and nature, Darwin said, was that civilized man cares for instead of exterminates the weaker members of the species. "The aid which we feel impelled to give to the helpless is mainly an incidental result of the instinct of sympathy," he declared, "which was originally acquired as part of the social instincts, but subsequently rendered . . . more tender and widely diffused. Nor could we check our sympathy, even at the urging of hard reason, without deterioration in the noblest part of our nature."[6] Spencer's equation between biological natural selection and what he called "social selection" led him to oppose all state aid to the poor, public education, health laws, and even public postal service. Sumner, a prototypical public intellectual who imbued thousands of the nation's future leaders with the ideology of untrammeled market capitalism during his tenure at Yale between 1872 and 1910, insisted that the business leaders of the Gilded Age had emerged through a process of selection equivalent to the triumph of the human species in nature. Furthermore, there were atheists and agnostics (on the political left as well as the right) who were convinced not only that the poor were poor because they were unfit but that natural selection had established a hierarchy of inferior and superior "races" (many of which would be called ethnic groups today). The statements of, among others, Elizabeth Cady Stanton and Margaret Sanger about the inferiority of immigrants are a continuing embarrassment to those who would like to think that their favorite social reformers, feminists, and antireligious dissenters were untainted by the prejudices of their era.

Broadly speaking, there are two divergent strains of American secular thought. One can be traced to the radical humanism of Tom Paine, who saw the separation of church and state not only as the guarantor of personal freedom of conscience but also as the foundation of a world in which inherited status and wealth would be replaced by merit and intellect as the dominant forces in the lives of individuals. Recognition of a common humanity, not tooth-and-claw competition, would create social progress. The other distinct current of American secularism begins with the social Darwinists of the nineteenth century and continues through the "objectivism" and exaltation of the Übermensch preached by the twentieth-century atheist and unregulated market idolator Ayn Rand. These diverging currents can also be found within the "new atheist" movement today, in which people often make a point of labeling themselves as either secular humanists, who are usually liberals, or skeptics, who are generally libertarian conservatives.* Even Ingersoll's friend Henry Ward Beecher, the champion of liberal Protestantism, delivered some astonishing perorations that made God sound like a social Darwinist. "God intended the great to be great and the little to be little," he preached in an 1877 sermon quoted approvingly in the *New York Times*. "I do not say that a dollar a day is enough to support a working man. But it is enough to support a man!"[7] After reading all of Ingersoll's published works and much of his private correspondence, I still find it difficult to explain the seeming inconsistency between his own place in the tradition of democratic secular humanism pioneered by Paine and his close personal relations with many social Darwinists. That paradox is the source of his singular importance in the history of American secularism, but it is also the reason why it has been difficult for historians to place him. Part of the explanation for Ingersoll's refusal to cast his lot with the social Darwinists surely lies in his big-hearted personality, because he also maintained friendly relations

*In American politics today, there are of course economic conservatives of the Randian strain who (unlike Rand) are not atheists but have embraced social conservatism as well. Representative Ron Paul and his son, Senator Rand Paul (named for you-know-who), are two prominent examples.

with men like Eugene V. Debs, a Socialist whose views on politics and economics could not have been farther from the allegiances of the wealthy. Ingersoll had met Debs in 1875, when the young Debs invited the Peoria lawyer— just beginning to "come out" as an agnostic—to speak before the Occidental Literary Club of Terra Haute, Indiana. The future Socialist candidate for president was so captivated by Ingersoll's talk that he not only accompanied him to the Terra Haute train station but bought himself a ticket and rode all the way to Cincinnati so that he and Ingersoll could continue their conversation.

No one, of course, is ever completely free of contemporary received opinion, but Ingersoll was far ahead of his time—farther ahead than many who agreed with his antireligious views—on a number of critical issues connected with but not solely defined by religious orthodoxy. The most important of these are racial equality, respect for varied ethnic groups, women's rights, and many disputes that would today fall within the realm of civil liberties. From a secular humanist perspective, Ingersoll was on the right side of nearly all of these issues. From the perspective of the social Darwinist-Randian secularists, Ingersoll was often on the wrong side—as he would be on the wrong side of Rand's devotees today.

After the Fourteenth Amendment was passed in 1868,

there is little to admire in the attitudes or actions of prominent white Americans, whatever their political affiliation, concerning the potential transformation of a recently enslaved race into a people who might make vital contributions to a nation that had, in its Faustian founding bargain, stripped them of human rights. That generalization applies to freethinkers, most of whom had been ardent abolitionists, as much as it does to any post-Reconstruction southern Democratic politician dedicated to the replacement of de jure with de facto slavery. While nearly all white freethinkers opposed slavery, that did not mean they were any more willing than the religiously orthodox to entertain the thought that blacks might be, even potentially, their social and intellectual equals.

In 1883, the Supreme Court handed down a decision that ought to be as infamous in the history of civil rights as *Plessy v. Ferguson,* which established the "separate but equal" doctrine, in 1896. The 1883 decision basically gutted the Civil Rights Act of 1875, which had outlawed racial discrimination in public accommodations and transportation.* Those provisions were declared unconstitutional, and the decision would stand as the basis of Jim Crow in everyday southern life for more than eighty years, until passage of the Public Accommodations Act of 1964. A week after the court handed down its ruling, with a sting-

---

*Decision 109 US3, October 15, 1883.

ing dissent by Justice John Marshall Harlan, hundreds
gathered for a protest meeting in Washington's Lincoln
Hall. Ingersoll was introduced as one of the main speakers
by Frederick Douglass and proceeded, unlike most leaders of his party, to eviscerate the court's logic. "This decision takes from seven millions of people the shield of the
Constitution," he said. "It leaves the best of the colored
race at the mercy of the meanest of the white. It feeds fat
the ancient grudge that vicious ignorance bears toward
race and color. It will be approved and quoted by hundreds of thousands of unjust men. The masked wretches
who, in the darkness of night, drag the poor negro from
his cabin, and lacerate with whip and thong his quivering
flesh, will, with bloody hands, applaud the Supreme Court.
The men who, by mob violence, prevent the negro from
depositing his ballot—those who with gun and revolver
drive him from the polls, and those who insult with vile
and vulgar words the inoffensive colored girl, will welcome
this decision with hyena joy. The basest will rejoice—the
noblest will mourn."[8] There could hardly have been a
more prescient statement, given that the high court's 1883
ruling stood largely unchallenged until the day in 1956
when a weary Rosa Parks sat down in the whites-only section of a bus in Birmingham, Alabama. Ingersoll also drew
a clear connection between a law that would deny people
the right to have a drink of water at a lunch counter and

the legal sanction of violence that denied an entire race the right to vote. In a statement directed specifically to his fellow Republicans, Ingersoll expressed indignation that "a man like Frederick Douglass can be denied entrance to a car, that the doors of a hotel can be shut in his face; that he may be prevented from entering a theatre—the idea that there shall be some ignominious corner into which such a man can be thrown by a decision of the Supreme Court."[9] He voiced the hope that the party of Lincoln, forged just before the Civil War, would realize that its mission had not ended with the formal abolition of slavery and would mount a new campaign for a public consensus on equal treatment of the races.

It is of more than passing interest that Ingersoll made his speech denouncing his party's abandonment of civil rights in Washington, which was as segregated well into the twentieth century as any city in the Deep South. He certainly knew that Douglass, attempting to enter the White House for a public reception after Lincoln's Second Inaugural Address, was detained by guards because he was a "person of color" and was admitted only on Lincoln's personal orders. Because freethought was primarily a northern phenomenon, many white freethinkers shared the enduring American delusion that racial discrimination was practiced mainly, if not exclusively, by southerners. Ingersoll, having spent most of his young manhood in the contested border areas between North and South, knew better.

What Ingersoll, like Voltaire and Paine before him, understood was the indivisibility of human rights, and he understood this not in spite of but precisely because of his disbelief in a deity who had supposedly "designed" the order of nature. The influence of social Darwinism had led many freethinkers to take a condescending view of the potential of new immigrant "races" in the United States—especially if, like the eastern European Jews, southern Italians, and Slavs who began pouring into the country after the Civil War, those people practiced their traditional (and strange to Americans of Anglo-Saxon origins) religions with the gusto and freedom allowed by the First Amendment. For female freethinkers, there was the added gall of the Fifteenth Amendment, which granted the vote to male ex-slaves but not to women of any color. Elizabeth Cady Stanton, at the first meeting of the National Woman Suffrage Association, personified the contempt with which some upper-class freethinkers regarded not only former black slaves but immigrants. "Think of Patrick and Sambo . . . and Yung Tung, who do not know the difference between a monarchy and a republic," she said, "who can not read the Declaration of Independence or Webster's spelling book, making laws for Lucretia Mott,

Ernestine L. Rose, and Anna E. Dickinson."[10] Even if it were true that many Patricks, Sambos, and Yung Tungs could not yet read or understand the Constitution, Ingersoll saw the problem as entirely solvable by public education.

Ingersoll's attitude toward Jewish immigration was consistent with his views about immigration in general. The Great Agnostic had no more use for religious Judaism than he did for Christianity (New York rabbis were just as offended by "Some Mistakes of Moses" as Catholic bishops and orthodox Protestant preachers were by Ingersoll's mockery of their belief that a god-man rose from the dead), but he correctly identified the Christian insistence that the Jews had killed their god as major source of anti-Semitism. "When I was a child," he recalled, "I was taught that the Jews were an exceedingly hard-hearted and cruel people, and that they were so destitute of the finer feelings that they had a little while before that time crucified the only perfect man who had appeared on earth; that this perfect man was also perfect God, and that the Jews had really stained their hands with the blood of the Infinite."[11]

In Ingersoll's time, however, the most virulent discrimination against immigrants was aimed not at any of the new arrivals from Europe but against Chinese, especially in the West. In 1882, Congress passed the first immigration law in the nation's history—the Chinese Exclusion

Act—specifically to bar the entrance of workers from a particular country. The Chinese had, of course, been welcome when there was a labor shortage and "coolies" were needed to build the transcontinental railroad. In 1892, the Exclusion Act was toughened under a law written by California representative Thomas J. Geary (the Geary whose memory is lionized in street names and other monuments throughout San Francisco). Under the Geary law, upheld by a 5–4 Supreme Court vote, all Chinese residents of the United States were required to carry a residence permit. Chinese were forbidden to bear witness in court should they be arrested for not carrying their internal "passport" and were denied bail. Once again, Ingersoll broke ranks with many in his party who supported both the Geary law (though Geary himself was a Democrat) and the earlier Exclusion Act, which was signed by Republican president Chester A. Arthur. As a lawyer, Ingersoll disagreed strongly with a statute that deprived Chinese of the legal protections enjoyed by all other immigrants. But his argument as a freethinker was based primarily on moral considerations and offered a powerful challenge to the social Darwinism preached by Spencer.

"The average American, like the average man of any country, has but little imagination," Ingersoll said. "People who speak a different language, or worship some other god, or wear clothing unlike his own, are beyond the horizon of his sympathy. He cares but little or nothing for the sufferings or misfortunes of those who are of a different complexion or another race. His imagination is not powerful enough to recognize the human being, in spite of peculiarities. . . . If these 'inferior people' claim equal rights he feels insulted, and for the purpose of establishing his own superiority tramples on the rights of the so-called inferior."[12] Immigrants from China, he said, should be treated in exactly the same way and should enjoy the same legal rights as immigrants whose skin color and culture were more familiar to Americans. In another statement highly unusual for his time, Ingersoll went on to compare the persecution of Chinese in the United States with the persecution of Jews in Tsarist Russia. "We are in the same business," he declared emphatically. "Our law is as inhuman as the order or ukase of the Czar."[13] Ingersoll considered the passage of laws that turned Chinese into a special category of American residents without constitutional rights as not only morally wrong but wrong in terms of American self-interest, since Chinese made up one-fourth of the human race and Americans surely wanted to trade with that country. "After all," Ingersoll said, "it pays to do right. This is a hard truth to learn— especially for a nation. A great nation should be bound by the highest conception of justice and honor. . . . It should remember that its responsibilities are in accordance with its power and intelligence."[14]

Ingersoll's rejection of the idea that women were, by nature, intellectually inferior to men—an article of faith for most men and most women in his era—was another of his distinguishing characteristics as a humanistic freethinker. The dedications of many volumes in Ingersoll's collected works emphasize his high opinion of the capabilities of women: Volume I, "To Eva A. Ingersoll, My Wife, A Woman without Superstition"; Volume II, "To Mrs. Sue M. Farrell, in law my sister, and in fact my friend"; Volume XII, "To My Daughters, Eva and Maud, whose hearts have never been hardened, whose imaginations have never been poisoned, and whose lives have never been cursed with the dogma of eternal fire." That Ingersoll was a family man who adored his wife and two daughters was well known, and his spotless domestic reputation— despite the best efforts of scandal-hungry reporters— frustrated those who wished to equate freethought with "free love." Ingersoll's twentieth-century biographers failed to recognize, probably because most of them were writing before the emergence of the second wave of American feminism in the 1970s, that Ingersoll held a radical view of women's rights and wrongs that went far beyond the suffragist movement of his time. In the battle over the subjugation of women, he sided with Stanton, who saw religion and centuries of religion-based law as the main cause of women's oppression, rather than with those who saw the vote itself as the ultimate remedy for all of women's ills. Like Stanton, Ingersoll viewed the franchise as necessary but not sufficient for women who wished to be not only the helpmates of men but the masters of their own lives. In this he resembled feminists of the 1970s and 1980s rather than the suffragists of his own time.

Before there were any reliable means of contraception, Ingersoll spoke about birth control as the precondition for women's liberation from servitude. He also understood that compulsory childbearing was used by both the church and individual men to stymie any other aspirations that women might possess. Ingersoll said emphatically, "Science must make woman the owner, the mistress of herself . . . must put it in the power of woman to decide for herself whether she will or will not become a mother." Women could never be truly free as long as they were forced to rely on the self-control of men to avoid unwanted pregnancy. "This is the solution of the whole question," Ingersoll emphasized. "This frees woman. The babes that are then born will be welcome. They will be clasped with glad hands to happy breasts. They will fill homes with light and joy." Those who considered the very mention of birth control obscene would be horrified by the possibility that women might choose whether to have children because involuntary motherhood guaranteed patriarchal control over all female behavior. Ingersoll correctly described the ethos of both men and women "who believe that slaves are purer, truer than the free, who believe that fear is a safer guide than knowledge, that only those are really good who obey the commands of others, and that ignorance is the soil in which the perfect, perfumed flower of virtue grows."[15]

Ingersoll was well aware that women, as a group, were more religious than men, but, in sharp contrast to Victorian moralists who considered the female sex "purer" than the male, he attributed feminine religiosity not to woman's higher nature but to her lack of education and utter economic dependency on her husband. In his preface to the prominent freethinker and feminist Helen H. Gardener's *Men, Women and Gods* (1885), Ingersoll said flatly, "Woman is not the intellectual inferior of man. She has lacked, not mind, but opportunity. . . . There were universities for men before the alphabet had been taught to women. At the intellectual feast, there was no place for wives and mothers. Even now they sit at the second table and eat the crusts and crumbs. The schools for women, at the present time, are just far enough behind those for men, to fall heirs to the discarded; on the same principle that when a doctrine becomes too absurd for the pulpit, it is given to the Sunday-school." Even worse, in Ingersoll's opinion, was the tendency of many husbands to regard religious superstition as the guardian of their wives' fidelity and their daughters' chastity. "These men think of priests as detectives in disguise," Ingersoll said, "and regard God as a policeman who prevents elopements."[16]

The result, in nineteenth-century America, was a union of religion and law in which women were expected to stay in a marriage even if they were regularly beaten and maimed by their husbands. In 1888, the *New York World* published a remarkable interview with Ingersoll in which he linked the right of a woman to divorce, and to obtain support for her children, with a case of domestic violence considered shocking even in a society where marital violence against women was rarely considered worthy of a headline. It seems that a man in the New York City borough of Queens had torn one of his wife's eyes out of its socket and then, a year later, returned home in a drunken rage and tore out the other eye. The blind wife could leave her husband and live separately from him, Ingersoll noted, but she would still be forced to stay legally married to her assailant and would "remain, for the rest of her days . . . a wife, hiding, keeping out of the way, secreting herself from the hyena to whom she was married." (From 1787 until 1967, adultery was the only ground for divorce in New York State—a policy upheld in the twentieth century largely as a result of strong lobbying by representatives of the powerful Catholic archdiocese of New York). In a forceful statement that sounds very much like the 1970s' feminist critique of male domestic violence, Ingersoll asked, "Must a woman in order to retain her womanhood become a slave, a serf, with a wild beast for a master, or with society for a master, or with a phantom for a master? Has not the married woman the right of self-defence? Is it not the duty of society to protect her from her husband? ... She may not remain in the same house with him, for fear that he may kill her. What, then, are their relations? Do they sustain any relation except that of hunter and hunted—that is, of tyrant and victim?"[17] Ingersoll did not hesitate to talk about other threats to women, such as rape, that were unmentionable in polite society. "It is hard to appreciate the dangers and difficulties that lie in wait for woman," he said. "Even in this Christian country of ours, no girl is safe in the streets of the city after the sun has gone down. *After all, the sun is the only god that has ever protected woman.* In the darkness she has been the prey of the wild beast in man" (italics mine).[18]

In the late nineteenth century, there were few women who dared to say, even if they thought, that patriarchal religion was a major obstacle to the full development of their sex. Stanton and Gardener were the exceptions, and

Stanton herself was pushed aside by the suffragist movement in the early 1890s after publishing her *Woman's Bible*, a strongly worded collection of essays by female scholars who criticized and reinterpreted the endless biblical passages claiming divine sanction for the inferiority of women. The suffragist movement began to make real headway in public opinion only when it discarded any broader critique of women's position in society and merged with the devoutly religious, female-led temperance movement, embodied by the Women's Christian Temperance Union. In the temperance movement, both women and men portrayed alcohol consumption as the only source of male violence against women and children.* Ingersoll, by contrast, viewed the connection between alcohol and violence within the home as only one more manifestation of the failure of both religion and government to uphold women's rights. Ingersoll was unimpressed by the argument that Christianity had elevated the status of women. He noted that Jesus "said not one word about the sacredness of home, the duties of the husband to the wife— nothing calculated to lighten the hearts of those who bear the saddest burdens of this life."[19] Jesus' first recorded miracle, turning water into wine at the wedding at Cana

---

*One important reason why the WCTU eventually joined the suffragist movement was that male state legislatures had repeatedly refused to pass laws establishing habitual drunkenness as a ground for divorce.

in response to his mother's request, impressed Ingersoll less than his insistence, while gathering his apostles, that men were obliged to forsake their earthly obligations, in the form of wife and family, to follow an itinerant preacher in the hills of Galilee.

Ingersoll was unusual in that he combined a basic belief in the intellectual equality of women and men with a romantic chivalry that owed more to his love of Shakespeare, Burns, Byron, and Keats than it did to contemporary social attitudes that placed women on a pedestal and required them to stay there. He often said that his favorite line of English verse was Shakespeare's "love is not love which alters when it alteration finds." In his most popular and frequently delivered lecture, "The Liberty of Man, Woman, and Child," Ingersoll followed up an ardent defense of equal rights for women with a reflection on love that expressed his romantic side and his feelings about his wife. "And do you know," he told his audiences, "it is a splendid thing to think that the woman you really love will never grow old to you. Through the wrinkles of time, through the mask of years, if you really love her, you will always see the face you loved and won. And a woman who really loves a man does not see that he grows old; he is not decrepit to her; she always sees the same gallant gentleman who won her hand and heart."[20] That mutual, lifelong love was Ingersoll's ideal did not prevent him from understanding that for millions of women, real life bore no resemblance to the ideal and that women's subsistence wages prevented most from exiting an intolerable marriage. Ingersoll viewed suffrage not as an end in itself, and not as a way to write puritanical religious concepts of "woman's place" into law, but as an essential first step toward the vastly needed improvement of wages and working conditions for women. "The question of wages for women is a thousand times more important than sending missionaries to China or to India," he said. "There is plenty for missionaries to do here. And by missionaries I do not mean gentlemen and ladies who distribute tracts or quote Scripture to people out of work. If we are to better the condition of men and women we must change their surroundings."[21] Ingersoll also anticipated a major theme in the feminist revival of the 1970s—the degree to which conventional morality had been used to justify the circumscription of all opportunities for women:

> There are so few occupations open to woman, so
> few things in which she can hope for independence,
> that to be thrown upon her own resources is almost
> equivalent to being cast away. Besides, she is an object
> of continual suspicion, watched not only by men but
> by women. If she does anything that other women are
> not doing, she is at once suspected, her reputation is

touched, and other women, for fear of being stained themselves, withdraw not only the hand of help, but the smile of recognition. A young woman cannot defend herself without telling the charge that has been made against her. This, of itself, gives a kind of currency to slander. To speak of the suspicion that has crawled across her path, to plant the seeds of doubt in other minds; to even deny it, admits that it exists. To be suspected, that is enough. There is no way of destroying this suspicion. There is no court in which suspicions are tried; no juries that can render verdicts of not guilty. Most women are driven at last to the needle, and this does not allow them to live; it simply keeps them from dying.[22]

The common thread in all of Ingersoll's thinking about social issues was secular humanism and its emphasis on the promotion of happiness in this world. Humanism distinguished him from the social Darwinist business leaders who shared his low opinion of religion but not his respect for workers and unlettered immigrants. "Secularism teaches us to be good here and now," he said. "I know nothing better than goodness. Secularism teaches us to be just here and now. It is impossible to be juster than just."[23] Just as Ingersoll was content to be called an atheist as well as an agnostic, he was perfectly happy to call secularism a religion—but it was a religion that he defined as the polar opposite of conventional faith, a system of thought that "trusts to individual effort, to energy, to intelligence, to observation and experience rather than the unknown and the supernatural. It desires to be happy on this side of the grave."[24]

Ingersoll defined secularism in a precise, down-to-earth fashion that eschewed broad philosophical generalizations—a tendency that led some later biographers to denigrate his abilities as a thinker even as they conceded his effectiveness as the greatest American popularizer of freethought, agnosticism, and evolution. He defined secularism as a way of life that "means food and fireside, roof and raiment, reasonable work and reasonable leisure, the cultivation of the tastes, the acquisition of knowledge, the enjoyment of the arts, and it promises for the human race comfort, independence, intelligence, and above all, liberty." A secularist society would mean "living for ourselves and each other; for the present instead of the past, for this world rather than another. . . . It is striving to do away with violence and vice, with ignorance, poverty and disease. . . . It does not believe in praying and receiving, but in earning and deserving."[25] A man who professed this humanistic secular creed could hardly have agreed with Spencer, who frequently said of the poor, "If they are sufficiently complete to live, they *do* live, and it is well that they should live. If they are not sufficiently complete to live, they die, and it is best that they should die."[26]

Ingersoll's philosophy was also rooted in the rapid, visible progress of technology and science, which had produced a general optimism about the future in late nineteenth-century America. He was not foolish enough to think that technology and science could do no wrong, but he did believe that only science, in its best forms, offered real alternatives to time-honored oppressive practices. This powerful strain in nineteenth-century American freethought impelled Ingersoll to predict that science would eventually break the chains that compulsory childbearing imposed on women of all social classes. But the underlying idea that women had a *right* to control of their own lives and bodies derives from the older Enlightenment value of universal human rights. Ingersoll was a proud heir to an Enlightenment tradition that, by the late nineteenth century, had been expanded by science beyond the material constraints of seventeenth- and eighteenth-century possibilities. He understood Darwin's theory of evolution not as a replacement for but as an addition to the Enlightenment philosophy of natural human rights: God need not be the father of all men for all men to be brothers. For Ingersoll, the common ancestry of human beings could never be reconciled with the social Darwinist conviction that the mighty were mighty and the serfs were serfs because they deserved to be so. And so he set out to reeducate his countrymen in a broader but entirely recognizable version of the Declaration of Independence's assertion that all men are endowed by their Creator with certain unalienable rights. This time, unalienable rights were not limited to men, or to whites, or to those at the top of the economic pyramid. And the Creator was replaced by creation itself.

V

Church and State

I deny the right of any man, of any number of men, of
any church, of any State, to put a padlock on the lips—
to make the tongue a convict. . . . Blasphemy is the word
that the majority hisses into the ear of the few.
—RGI, May 19, 1887, at the New Jersey blasphemy
trial of C. B. Reynolds

The propinquity in time of America's revolutionary generation to the worst manifestations of theocracy in the Old World is utterly ignored today by the historical revisionists of the religious right, who claim that the United States was founded as a Christian nation. But the power of religion-based law, as enforced by the state, was very much on the minds of the framers of the world's first secular constitution. When the Constitution was being written in Philadelphia in 1787, only two decades had passed since the horrifying execution in France of nineteen-year-old Jean-François Lefevre, Chevalier de la Barre, for blasphemy—a case, publicized by Voltaire, that shocked the educated world. This famous case was tried—if the word "trial" even applies—in Normandy, in the town of

Abbeville. A crucifix had been defaced, and the chevalier, who was known in the area for a certain wildness and propensity for singing bawdy anti-clerical songs, was charged with blasphemy. An important piece of evidence against him was his possession of a copy of Voltaire's *Dictionnaire Philosophique Portatif,* an anthology including many articles attacking the Catholic Church.* The young nobleman was sentenced to the customary punishment—being burned—after having his right hand cut off and his tongue cut out; Voltaire's book was burned along with him. The defendant refused to confess or name any other young men who had participated—even after being tortured for the final hour before his execution (again, as mandated by law), and the sentence was then carried out. The clerics and government magistrates, after cutting off the hand as specified in the sentence, showed unexpected mercy by not cutting out the young nobleman's tongue before the auto da fé.†

The men who framed the Constitution were mindful

---

*Voltaire's *Dictionnaire*, published in 1764, was not a dictionary of words but did classify its articles and subjects in alphabetical order—a practice introduced during the Enlightenment. It included many articles dealing with the church's history of prosecuting religious dissidents for heresy and blasphemy. It was designed to be more compact, and therefore more easily accessible, than previously published alphabetically arranged volumes.

†Details of the execution vary in different accounts (including those by Voltaire himself). In some versions, the young chevalier was beheaded before his body was burned. The burning of the book along with the body, dead or alive, is reported in every version.

and fearful of the history of state-enforced religious power in Europe and were determined that the blueprint for the new national government would provide no sanction for such actions—even though most state governments did have laws privileging particular religious denominations. But the framers made no mention of God, even the deistic "providence," in the preamble and explicitly prohibited religious tests for federal office in Article 6, Section 3—although numerous states retained such prohibitions in their laws into the 1840s. Many states also had blasphemy laws, dating from the early 1800s, on their books, but such laws were rarely enforced. If local defenders of the faith became agitated, however, they could invoke the old laws and try to enforce them. That is what brought Robert Ingersoll to court in Morristown, New Jersey, to defend freethinker C. B. Reynolds, who had distributed a pamphlet denying the infallibility and divine authorship of the Bible, as Thomas Paine had (with greater literary skill) more than a century earlier.

Reynolds was one of the traveling lecturers who spoke throughout the country in tents provided by donors to the American Secular Union, the best-known national freethought organization of the era. The tents were needed because most lecture halls would not rent space to antireligious speakers (unless the speaker was Ingersoll, who always sold out the house and made money for the godly proprietor). Appearing in the "freethought tent" erected in the small town of Boonton, New Jersey, Reynolds had to flee as a stone-throwing mob began to vandalize the canvas structure (which was ultimately shredded). Then he moved on to distribute more pamphlets attacking the Bible in Morristown, not far from the stretch of the Delaware River where George Washington made his famous crossing on Christmas Eve of 1776. The Morristown pamphlet had a cover that particularly enraged Methodists and Catholics, because it showed Reynolds literally trying to cast pearls before Methodist and Catholic swine pictured in the foreground. Reynolds was charged under a statute dating from the colonial era, which made blasphemy a crime punishable by a year of imprisonment or a fine of two hundred dollars. In his summation, Ingersoll emphasized the descent of the New Jersey law from the kinds of laws that had decreed the death penalty for blasphemy—not in the Middle Ages but at the very time the United States was becoming a nation. Such laws, Ingersoll said, identified any man who disagreed with some aspect of orthodox doctrine (whether orthodox Protestantism or orthodox Catholicism) "and took that poor honest wretch—while his wife wept—while his children clung to his hands—to the public square, drove a stake in the ground, put a chain or two about him, lighted the fagots, and let the wife whom he loved and his little children see the flames climb around his limbs." Even though the penalty might be less harsh, Ingersoll emphasized, "the same spirit made this detestable, infamous, devilish" New Jersey law.[1]

The Reynolds trial, widely publicized in New York because Morristown is located only thirty miles from the city, did not attract the same level of national publicity that the Scopes trial would forty years later. What the trials had in common was that they were perceived, at least by intellectuals and some business leaders, as the last stand of rigid religious belief that, even though it might still be enshrined in old laws, had little to do with everyday contemporary life and social institutions. As Ingersoll noted in his summation, the last person imprisoned for blasphemy in the United States, the Universalist minister-turned-freethinker Abner Kneeland, had been jailed in Boston nearly a half-century earlier in 1838. Kneeland, who had been arrested for stating that the Christian god of the Universalists was "nothing more than a chimera," was unsuccessful in a defense claiming that he was not an atheist but a pantheist. (He served sixty days in jail and moved on to Iowa, where he founded a little-known utopian community named Salubria.)

Ingersoll's chief argument in the trial was that the old blasphemy law violated the 1844 New Jersey state constitution, which, like most state constitutions, guaranteed freedoms of speech and religion along the lines of the federal constitution's First Amendment. Although the blasphemy law had not been enforced for most of the nineteenth century, Ingersoll reminded the jurors, the statute had nevertheless been allowed to "slumber" on the books. "You inherited it from your ignorant ancestors, and they inherited it from their savage ancestors," he explained. "The people of New Jersey were heirs of the mistakes and the atrocities of ancient England."[2] It should be recalled that in Ingersoll's time, the equal protection clause of the Fourteenth Amendment, ratified in 1868, was not used to challenge state laws that conflicted with the Bill of Rights; the only argument he could make was that the New Jersey blasphemy law violated the state's own constitution. (As evinced by his condemnation of the 1883 Supreme Court decision repealing the federal civil rights act, Ingersoll held to a broad interpretation of the national Constitution.) Ingersoll concluded his defense by appealing to the jury's patriotism and expressing the fervent wish "that it will never be necessary again, under the flag of the United States—that flag for which has been shed the best and bravest blood of the world—under that flag maintained by Washington, by Jefferson, by Franklin and by Lincoln—under that flag in defence of which New Jersey poured out her best and bravest blood—I hope that it will never be necessary again for a man to stand before a jury and plead for the Liberty of Speech."[3]

According to the *New York Times*, "As Colonel Ingersoll left the room, a throng pressed after him to offer him congratulations. One old man said: 'Colonel Ingersoll, I am a Presbyterian pastor, but I must say that was one of the noblest speeches in defence of liberty I ever heard! Your hand, sir; your hand!'"[4] The jury, however, was not convinced. The outcome of the Reynolds trial clearly reflected the ambivalence of the court about religion-based law and the separation of church and state. The jurors returned a verdict of guilty, but the judge, unwilling to be recorded in history as the man who imprisoned an American citizen for blasphemy for the first time in fifty years, imposed a fine of only twenty-five dollars. He also assessed seventy-five dollars in court costs, which were paid by Ingersoll, who had already donated his own legal services.

The prosecution of Reynolds for blasphemy underscores the shortness of the period, as historical time is measured, between an era when a man might be imprisoned or even killed for expressing disbelief in a particular religion and an era in which, even though freethought was not generally accepted, it also seemed anachronistic to severely punish anyone for ridiculing the idea of a deity. In his summation to the jury, Ingersoll stressed the antiquated nature of any blasphemy charge, but he was certainly well aware that a century, or a half-century, not only *sub specie aeternitatis* but in an ordinary man's life, was a very short time for society to embrace an intellectual and political shift as important as the acceptance of man's right to scoff at God.

In its national constitution, America had turned its back on theocracy swiftly but without violence—a shift that contrasted sharply with the bloody religious strife that had roiled seventeenth-century England and would consume the French Revolution during the Jacobin terror. But the pace of religious change in the new nation was uneven, affected not only by the tension between the federal republic and states' rights but by an education gap between the North and South that widened as slavery fostered resistance to both public schooling and any science that challenged the Bible. Those who claim today that the founders never really meant to separate church and state argue that the framers of the Constitution expected nearly all matters of religion, and government relations with religion, to be determined by the states. According to this logic, little importance should be attached to the omission of God from the Constitution, the prohibition of religious tests for national office, or the careful provision that officeholders be allowed to "swear or affirm" their allegiance to the United States. (The word "affirm" was specifically intended to allow declarations of allegiance by those who did not wish to "swear on the Bible.") In this view, the body of the Constitution and the First Amendment were designed only to protect religion from government—not government from religion.

The opponents of church-state separation are partly right: the founders did indeed know that there was an existing crazy-quilt of state laws favoring religion in general and, in many instances, one established religion. At the time the national constitution was ratified, the Massachusetts state constitution—much to John Adams's dismay—prohibited both Jews and Catholics from holding public office. Delaware required officeholders to affirm their belief in the Holy Trinity. New York allowed Jews and Protestants, but not Catholics, to hold office. What the founders did by leaving God out of the Constitution, and making it clear that religious belief was not a condition for holding federal office, was announce that the new *nation* was going to do things differently. There was no doubt in the minds of those who wanted a constitution that paid customary deference to the deity as the source of political power that the omission of God from the document did represent a momentous departure from the idea and ideal of a Christian nation. The Reverend John M. Mason, a fiery New York Federalist who did not share Washington's and Adams's liberality in religious matters, decried the absence of God in the Constitution as "an omission which no pretext whatever can palliate." He warned his fellow

Americans that "we will have every reason to tremble, lest the Governor of the universe, who will not be treated with indignity by a people more than individuals, overturn from its foundations the fabric we have been rearing, and crush us to atoms in the wreck."[5]

Moreover, many of the founders, including Jefferson, Madison, and Adams, hoped that the new federal constitution would encourage the states to revise their religiously based laws. Their hope was partly fulfilled. Between 1789 and 1792, five of the original thirteen states changed their religious laws to reflect the more secular values of the Constitution. It took the other original states decades longer to arrive at anything approaching the Constitution's example. Massachusetts, still bound to its Puritan heritage, did not remove all religious restrictions on holding public office until 1833, and Connecticut took another decade to allow Jews to run for office.* But new states joining the union, as the framers had hoped, generally took the federal constitution as their model on relations between church and state. Nevertheless, many "sleeper" religion-based laws, like New Jersey's blasphemy statute, remained on the books.

The society in which Ingersoll set out to remind his

---

*One of Adams's greatest disappointments in old age was his inability, at the Massachusetts constitutional convention in 1820, to persuade the delegates to grant equal legal rights to Jews.

countrymen of the nation's most secular revolutionary traditions was, of course, characterized by a much higher level of religious pluralism than the early republic. The post–Civil War influx of East European Jews and Roman Catholics had reminded the Protestant religious establishment of the predictions of many orthodox eighteenth-century ministers that the godless constitution would, in theory, allow anyone—including atheists, Jews, and those Protestant theological flip-floppers, Unitarians and Universalists—to serve as president. There was also enormous concern about the growing political influence of Roman Catholics in the nation's large cities. These fears about religious pluralism played an important role in the repeated demands by mainstream Protestant organizations for a Christian amendment, like the one presented to Abraham Lincoln, to remedy the primal religious omission of the founders. (The American Catholic hierarchy, well aware of the Protestant American majority's fear of Rome and "popery," did not make such demands at the time.)

Ingersoll used every possible public platform to remind Americans why the founders had written a godless constitution in the first place. In response to one of the many ministerial pleas for a godly constitution since Lincoln had evaded the issue in 1864, Ingersoll noted that "if there is to be an acknowledgment of God in the Constitution, the question naturally arises as to which God is to have this honor."

Shall we select the God of the Catholics—he who has established an infallible church presided over by an infallible pope, and who is delighted with certain ceremonies and placated by prayers uttered in exceedingly common Latin? Is it the God of the Presbyterians with the Five Points of Calvinism, who is ingenious enough to harmonize necessity and responsibility, and who in some way justifies himself for damning most of his own children? Is it the God of the Puritans, the enemy of joy—of the Baptist, who is great enough to govern the universe, and small enough to allow the destiny of a soul to depend on whether the body it inhabited was immersed or sprinkled?

What God is it proposed to put in the Constitution? Is it the God of the Old Testament, who was a believer in slavery and who justified polygamy? If slavery was right then, it is right now; and if Jehovah was right then, the Mormons are right now. Are we to have the God who issued a commandment against all art—who was the enemy of investigation and of free speech? . . . What court, what tribunal of last resort, is to define this God, and who is to make known his will? In His presence, laws passed by men will be of no value. The decisions of courts will be as nothing. But who is to make known the will of this supreme God? Will there be a supreme tribunal composed of priests?[6]

Ingersoll had two major concerns about separation of church and state. First, he feared that in an expanding and expansive society that included people of more varied cultures and beliefs than the founders could ever have imagined, the most retrograde representatives of orthodox Protestantism would attempt to solidify their political and economic power by laying claim to a religion-based political authority denied by the Constitution. Second, he anticipated that the Catholic Church would press for more laws in conformity with its doctrines as the number of American Catholics increased. This concern intensified as Catholics began to finance the nation's first large parochial school system as an alternative to public education. Ingersoll saw the Catholic opposition to free public schooling and its suspicion of science as particularly harmful and noted that the Vatican respected the religious liberty of others only in areas where Catholics were a minority.

But Ingersoll also had a low opinion of the curriculum in American public schools when it came to teaching students about either freedom of conscience or the separation of church and state in American history. If public schools and their teachers were doing a good job of representing the secular side of history, Ingersoll argued, the jurors in the Reynolds blasphemy trial would have understood the connection between an eighteenth-century auto da fé and a nineteenth-century imposition of even a small fine for distributing a pamphlet ridiculing the Bible.

For the Great Agnostic, the relative obscurity of Thomas Paine in the second half of the American nineteenth century was nothing less than a crime against the true history of the United States. Paine's writings were, by then, much better known among the educated classes in England than in America. "These are the times that try men's souls"— the opening line of *The Crisis Papers*—may have been more familiar to nineteenth-century American schoolchildren than it is to children today, but Paine himself was a touchy and largely unexplored subject. The pre-revolutionary call to arms "Common Sense" sold more than half a million copies in the colonies in the mid-1770s. Paine received no money for his famous revolutionary pamphlets, because he allowed them to be published and circulated freely as his contribution to American independence. As Ingersoll noted in his standard speech on Paine, "no one stood higher in America" at the successful conclusion of the Revolution than the author of *The Crisis Papers*. "The best, the wisest, the most patriotic, were his friends and admirers," Ingersoll recalled, "and had he been thinking only of his own good he might have rested from his toil and spent the remainder of his life in comfort and in ease." This alternative Paine could have remained "what the world is pleased to call 'respectable.' He could have died surrounded by clergymen, warriors and statesmen. At his death there would have been an imposing funeral, miles of carriages, civic societies, salvos of artillery, a nation in mourning, and, above all, a splendid monument covered with lies. He chose rather to benefit mankind."[7]

The benefit to mankind, as outlined by Ingersoll for his audiences, was Paine's exploration of the religious tyranny that had always been indispensable to political tyranny: "He knew that the throne skulked behind the altar, and both behind a pretended revelation from God."[8] Living out his credo that "the world is my country, and to do good my religion," Paine resided and wrote in both England and France after the American Constitution was ratified. Threatened with a possible charge of treason, Paine was forced to flee England after publication, in 1791, of the anti-monarchist *The Rights of Man*, but his writings were so popular in France that he was elected to the revolutionary National Assembly in 1792. Soon he was in trouble again, imprisoned, and in danger of being put to death, because of his principled opposition to capital punishment. Even though Paine was the most passionate of anti-monarchists, he opposed the execution of King Louis XVI on the ground that the state degraded itself and, in a democracy, its citizens by claiming and exercising the authority to take human life. Ingersoll, like nearly all freethinkers, opposed both the death penalty and torture because such punishments were historically rooted in the idea that since God has the power of life and death, the government, as the deity's representative on earth, could also lay claim to that power.*

The death penalty was prescribed for hundreds of offenses in the Old Testament, Ingersoll noted, and Christian countries followed suit until the end of the eighteenth century. He described the prohibition of "cruel and unusual punishment," enshrined in the Bill of Rights, as another secular concept. By the late nineteenth century, the death penalty was considered too cruel and unusual to be

---

*Supreme Court Associate Justice Antonin Scalia, a strong supporter of the death penalty, explicitly made this argument in a speech delivered at the University of Chicago Divinity School in 2002 and tellingly titled "God's Justice and Ours." Democracy, Scalia argues, is responsible for the rise of opposition to the death penalty in the twentieth century. "Few doubted the morality of the death penalty in the age that believed in the divine right of kings," Scalia adds. That is undeniably true but is hardly a constitutionally viable argument for capital punishment imposed by a modern state: one might as well argue that human sacrifice is acceptable because in many primitive cultures, few doubted the morality of crushing skulls in order to place them in the foundations of temples as a rite of sanctification and purification.

imposed for such crimes as horse thievery—though not for rape. Murder and treason, however, remained capital crimes in every state. Like Paine, Ingersoll opposed the death penalty not out of pity for criminals but because he thought that such punishments debased the people whose government claimed the right to murder—whatever the form of government. "Search the records of the world," Ingersoll insisted, "and you will find but few sublimer acts than that of Thomas Paine voting against the king's death. He, the hater of despotism, the abhorrer of monarchy, the champion of the rights of man, the republican, accepting death to save the life of a deposed tyrant—of a throneless king. This was the last grand act of his political life—the sublime conclusion of his political career."[9]

The Age of Reason was widely read in the 1790s because it was written in the same direct, commonsensical language as Paine's revolutionary pamphlets and was therefore understandable—unlike abstruse theological arguments in defense of orthodox religion and union between church and state—to anyone who could read. "The 'Age of Reason' has liberalized us all," Ingersoll said. "It put arguments in the mouths of the people; it put the church on the defensive; it enabled somebody in every village to corner the parson; it made the world wiser, and the church better; it took power from the pulpit and divided it among the pews."[10]

Ingersoll often told the story of Paine's near-death of an ulcer in the Luxembourg prison before the U.S. government intervened to obtain his release. He was not allowed to return to the United States until 1802, after Thomas Jefferson was elected president, and Jefferson was sharply criticized for allowing the revolutionary hero—now denigrated as an infidel—to come home on an American navy ship. As Ingersoll had noted in one of his early freethought orations in 1870, Paine was forced to eat "the bitter bread of sorrow" for expressing his skepticism about religion. "His friends were untrue to him because he was true to himself and true to them. He lost the respect of what is called society, but kept his own. His life is what the world calls failure and what history calls success."[11]

Only in 1892 would Paine receive his full due as both a revolutionary writer and a religious skeptic, in a magisterial two-volume biography by Moncure Daniel Conway, a minister-turned-freethinker. This book, which received considerable attention because it was published at the height of the nineteenth-century freethought movement, remains an indispensible source for Paine scholars today. Conway concluded his biography with an account of the removal of Paine's skeleton from his obscure grave in New Rochelle, New York, and the transportation of his bones to England. "There is a legend that Paine's little

finger was left in America," Conway wrote, "a fable, perhaps of his once small movement, now stronger than the
loins of the bigotry that refused him a vote or a grave in
the land he so greatly served. As to his bones, no man
knows the place of their rest to this day. His principles
rest not."[12] Ingersoll, in an 1892 review of Conway's biography, rejoiced that at long last, "the real history of
Thomas Paine, of what he attempted and accomplished,
of what he taught and suffered, has been intelligently,
truthfully and candidly given to the world. Henceforth
the slanderer will be without excuse."[13] (In an 1888 biography of the Federalist politician Gouverneur Morris,
Theodore Roosevelt had described Paine as a "filthy little
atheist." Morris, as it happens, was President George
Washington's minister to France in 1793, when Paine was
arrested for his opposition to the execution of Louis XVI.
A fierce critic of Paine's religious and economic views,
Morris misled the French with the claim that the new
United States government did not recognize the British-
born Paine's American citizenship. At the same time, Mor-
ris told Washington—who, though he too disliked Paine's
economic radicalism, recognized his debt to the author of
The Crisis Papers—that everything was being done to obtain Paine's release from Luxembourg Prison. Only when
James Monroe, a freethinker, replaced Morris in Paris did

the American government apply pressure to obtain Paine's freedom. He had spent nine months in solitary confinement and nearly died of an ulcer.)

Like the public's reaction against Paine in the early 1900s, the intense, divided response to Ingersoll at the end of the century was ignited not only by the continuing tension between religious power in American society and legal separation of church and state but also by the expanding influence of secularism even among the religious. In this respect, the religious landscape of the United States during the Gilded Age was not dissimilar from our own: the influence of biblically literal evangelicalism was growing even as mainstream Protestantism struggled to accommodate science and modernism by viewing the stories in both the Christian and Jewish Bibles in a metaphoric rather than a literal sense.

In the nineteenth century, despite the much stronger influence of Protestantism and the growing influence of Catholicism, the formidable nature of the challenge posed by contemporary science, especially biology and geology, to biblical literalism may be inferred from the fact that the young William Jennings Bryan, while a student at Illinois College, wrote a letter to Ingersoll asking for his advice about dealing with the emerging contradictions between his education and his faith. This approach by Bryan to

Ingersoll is not entirely surprising, since Bryan was born in 1860 in Marion County, Illinois, where Ingersoll, like Lincoln, began his career as a lawyer. By the time Bryan was a college student in the 1870s, Ingersoll had also begun his career as an opponent of organized religion.* The man who would one day be known as "the great commoner" had heard the great agnostic speak, although Bryan himself would follow the more histrionic and sentimental style of evangelical preachers, better suited to his message than Ingersoll's matter-of-fact way of speaking to an audience.[14] The connection between old-time religion and politics, however, was the reverse of today's close relationship between religion and economic conservatism. Bryan was the leader of the entwined forces of economic and religious populism until his death in 1925 (shortly after the Scopes trial). His famous 1896 "cross of gold" speech had embodied the philosophical linkage between turn-of-the-century evangelical religion and the desire for economic (though not racial) justice. Bryan would undoubtedly have been astonished had someone told him in the 1890s that a century in the future, Americans who upheld the literal truth of Genesis would be equally com-

---

*Ingersoll apparently never answered the letter, although his correspondence contains many personal replies to inquiries like Bryan's. One can only wonder if a direct engagement with Ingersoll would have altered the mindset that produced Bryan's lifelong commitment to the defense of literal biblical faith.

mitted to the idea that the rich should pay lower taxes and that corporations should be treated as people.

The great religious and political paradox of the golden age of freethought was that even as the proportion of freethinkers and "religious liberals" increased, politicians were required to pay greater obeisance to religion than they had been either in the founding generation or at various earlier points in the nineteenth century. President Andrew Jackson, at a time when Paine's reputation had been obliterated except among freethinkers, declared that "Thomas Paine needs no monument made with hands" because he "has erected a monument in the hearts of all lovers of liberty." Lincoln—unlike William McKinley during the Spanish-American War—had explicitly rejected the claim that "God is on our side" during the Civil War. He pointedly observed in his Second Inaugural Address that both sides "read the same Bible, and pray to the same God; and each invokes his aid against the other," adding that the prayers of both the North and the South could not be answered and that neither had been answered fully.

For Ingersoll, the primary danger of entanglement between religion and politics was that invoking divine authority would simply shut down discussion on controversial issues. The requirement that politicians be religious, or at least appear to be religious, ruled out a significant group of independent thinkers from office. Ingersoll decried the

public religiosity required of politicians in a statement
that is just as applicable today as it was then.

> At present, the successful office-seeker is a good deal
> like the centre of the earth; he weighs nothing him-
> self, but draws everything else to him. There are so
> many societies, so many churches, so many isms, that
> it is almost impossible for an independent man to
> succeed in a political career. Candidates are forced
> to pretend that they are Catholics with Protestant
> proclivities, or Christians with liberal tendencies, or
> temperance men who now and then take a glass of
> wine, or, that although not members of any church
> their wives are, and that they subscribe liberally to all.
> The result of all this is that we reward hypocrisy and
> elect men entirely destitute of real principle; and this
> will never change until the people become grand
> enough to do their own thinking.[15]

A candidate's religious outlook, in Ingersoll's opinion,
should be an entirely private matter. "If we were in a
storm at sea," he said, "with deck wave-washed and masts
strained and bent with storm, and it was necessary to reef
the top sail, we certainly would not ask the brave sailor
who volunteered to go aloft, what his opinion was on the
five points of Calvinism."[16] Ingersoll felt that the churches
of his day were becoming politicized and correctly pre-

dicted that it would not be long until religious institutions would "divide as sharply upon political, as upon theological questions."

Then as now, American religious conservatives favored the use of government power to enforce specific, religiously based moral principles. The Comstock Laws, used to define both Walt Whitman's poetry and advertisements for contraceptives as obscene, were backed by the most conservative Protestant denominations and the Catholic Church. Ingersoll had no particular interest in the obscenity issue per se—he was personally repelled by images that degraded women—but he argued that the Comstock Laws were being used to persecute editors and writers of publications like the *Truth Seeker* for unpopular antireligious and political views under the guise of obscenity. Since Ingersoll believed that women could be truly liberated only when science enabled them to decide whether to have children, he could hardly have considered advertisements for (largely ineffective) contraceptives obscene.* Comstock not only hounded the editors of freethought publications but played a personal role in the use of the law to prevent distribution of Whitman's *Leaves of Grass* for several decades after Whitman first self-published it

---

*The idea that Vaseline was an effective contraceptive persisted, alas, well into the twentieth century—especially among the young—and was surely responsible for a fair number of teen pregnancies.

in 1855. Ingersoll had long considered Whitman the greatest American poet and viewed the government-sponsored
campaign to obstruct distribution of his work as a dis-
graceful example of religious interference, backed by the
state, with liberties guaranteed by the First Amendment.

Finally, Ingersoll considered the separation of church and
state in free public schools (and by free, he meant in both
the intellectual and financial senses of the word) of ultimate importance. Born at a time when Americans were an
overwhelmingly Protestant people, his main concern in
the early years of his emergence as the "Great Agnostic"
was the lingering influence of Calvinism in public education. Ingersoll was no fan of primers that used "in Adam's
fall, we sinned all" to teach children to read. His daughters, Eva and Maud, were mainly educated by private tu-
tors because the Ingersolls did not want their children
exposed to religious dogma as a condition of teaching
(although the Ingersoll girls, like their parents, were
well schooled in the Bible as a work of literature and
philosophy).

   As the great migration from southern and eastern Europe continued in the 1880s and 1890s, Ingersoll became
more concerned about the Catholic Church's push for
the kind of state support that Catholic schools received in
many European countries. This freethought position was

descended directly from the 1786 Virginia Act for Establishing Religious Freedom, written by James Madison and passed in response to a proposal that property taxes be levied for the support of teachers of the Christian religion in common schools. Ingersoll was not happy that some Protestant theological conventions had remained embedded in many public schools throughout the nation (an argument the Catholic Church used in its unsuccessful attempts to gain public tax support for its own schools), but his solution was to get all religious teaching out of the public schools—not to provide state support for alternative religious schools. (In the nineteenth century, Jews did not figure in this debate because immigrant Jews—even the most religious—were simply happy to have access to a public education that had been denied them in most Catholic and Protestant regions of eastern Europe and Russia. In the post–World War II twentieth century, Jewish organizations would adopt the old freethought position that remnants of Christian education had no place in public schools.)

Ingersoll believed that education was the best investment government could make at any level and still regretted the fact that in the early republic, Congress had yielded to pressure by denominational colleges (which Harvard, Yale, and other prestigious institutions still were in the early 1800s). Congress also rejected a legacy left by

President George Washington, upon his death in 1799, for the establishment of a publicly supported, secular national university. Ingersoll considered the schools in his own city, New York, to be poorly supported by local and state government in the 1890s. "Many of them are small, dark, unventilated and unhealthy," he said in an interview in the *New York World*. "They should be the finest buildings in the city. It would be far better for the Episcopalians to build a university than a cathedral."* He asserted that we "need far more schoolhouses than we have, and while money is being wasted in a thousand directions, thousands of children are left to be educated in the gutter. It is far cheaper to build schoolhouses than prisons, and it is much better to have scholars than convicts."[17] For Ingersoll, it was a given that tax-supported schools should be thoroughly secular and teach only what could be deduced "about this world, about this life." Like so many of the causes he championed, Ingersoll's vision of secular American education, and of a nation in which the line between church and state is clearly drawn and respected by all, remains a work-in-progress.

---

*Ingersoll was referring to the Cathedral of St. John the Divine, the construction of which began in 1892.

VI

Reason and Passion

Not till the sun excludes you, do I exclude you.
—Walt Whitman, "To a Common Prostitute"

Allusions to this famous, once-scandalous Whitman poem occur many times, in many contexts, in Robert Ingersoll's lectures, essays, and interviews. His attachment to this particular line of American verse explains, on an even deeper level than his advocacy of science, secularism, and the separation of church and state, why the word "great" was appended to the informal title used not only by his admirers but by his more open-minded critics. Then as now, freethinkers, secularists, agnostics, and atheists—whatever they call themselves or others choose to call them—were often portrayed by their religious enemies as cool, uncaring skeptics who had nothing but contempt for the emotional needs served by religion. If the free-thinkers were right, and there was no benevolent creator, no reason for suffering, no eternal life, what, then, would comfort the grieving and the afflicted? Even the tough-minded suffragist and agnostic Susan B. Anthony wondered whether "if it be true that we die like the flower, leaving behind only the fragrance . . . what a delusion has the race ever been in—what a dream is the life of man."[1] To such existential questions, Ingersoll did not offer reason and the search for truth as their own rewards (although he did consider them greater blessings than any promise of eternal life). Instead, he offered the emotional argument that finitude is what gives this life meaning. In a graveside eulogy for a friend's child, he told the mourners, "If those we press and strain within our arms could never die, perhaps that love would wither from the earth. May be this common fate treads from out the paths between our hearts and the weeds of selfishness and hate. And I had rather live and love where death is king, than have eternal life where love is not. . . . They who stand with breaking hearts around this little grave, need have no fear. The larger and nobler faith in all that is, and is to be, tells us that death, even at its worst, is only the perfect rest."[2] By referring to faith in what "is to be," Ingersoll was not implying that he believed in eternal life or other-worldly reunions with loved ones—even though, as a proper agnostic, he simply maintained that there was no evidence of an afterlife and that the ancient longing of human beings for immortality had no bearing on the question. Ingersoll's eulogies, which always emphasized that the dead, in a state of "perfect rest," could feel no pain and sorrow, appealed to many liberal religious believers as well as freethinkers, because one of the distinctive characteristics of modernizing forces within American Protestantism was less emphasis on divine punishment.*

In all of the earthly matters he considered most important, Ingersoll saw no conflict between emotion and reason, between passion and rationality—unless emotion and passion were subordinated to rigid ideology of either a religious or secular nature. His insistence that passion and reason must work in tandem for the good of humanity made him unusual in his own time and explained why he could never accept total determinism of any kind—whether social Darwinism on the right or European socialist ideology on the left. That Ingersoll himself espoused many causes supported by American socialists, like the eight-hour workday, attested to both the humanism and the pragmatism integral to his idea of how reason should operate in society. If compassion and a sense of common humanity were not reason enough for owners to

---

*The downgrading of the flames of hell worked. A 2008 poll conducted by the Pew Forum on Religion and Public Life showed that while 74 percent of Americans believe in heaven, only 59 percent believe in hell.

treat workers fairly, Ingersoll argued, the self-interest of capitalists was served by decent conditions for labor. A consultation with God or his self-proclaimed representatives on earth was neither required nor useful in the continuing struggle to devise a more just and productive human environment.

In this biography, I have paid scant attention to the philosophical debates between Ingersoll and contemporary theologians, which were published in intellectual journals and aroused considerable interest among the same kind of people who now attend debates between atheist authors like Sam Harris and Richard Dawkins and their religious critics. Such debates have always attracted audiences composed mainly of those who are already committed to one religious or antireligious position and whose minds are unlikely to be changed by anything they hear. Ingersoll's genius as an advocate for freethought lay not in his ability to best clerical antagonists in arguments about the logical impossibility of the Holy Trinity (although, as a minister's son, he possessed the theological armament needed for such debates) but in his impassioned portrayal of decent behavior, of goodness, as an obligation of human beings toward one another simply by virtue of their common humanity.

When he made his argument for what he called the
"gospel of humanity," Ingersoll often turned to the arts.
His love and knowledge of music, the theater, and literature was deep, and his contributions to the arts generous,
as evinced by the letters of condolence Mrs. Ingersoll received from hundreds of actors and musicians, including
the president of the American Federation of Musicians.
Throughout the Ingersolls' thirteen years in Manhattan,
where they settled in 1886 mainly because it offered a
livelier cultural environment than Washington, their hospitality to writers, actors, and musicians was legendary.
Their last residence, a townhouse adjoining Gramercy
Park, was located just around the corner from The Players' Club, founded in 1888 by their friend Edwin Booth,
the foremost American Shakespearean actor of his time.*

For Ingersoll, evidence-based science did not occupy
a separate category from the greatest works of painting,
sculpture, literature, and music: all were glorious evidence
of the best human achievements, rendered even more pre-
cious because they were the products of natural evolution
and human inspiration rather than supernatural creation
and divine design. Unlike his more conservative contemporaries, whose reverence for the arts and artists did not
include many of the masterpieces of the preceding half-

---

*Booth was the brother of Lincoln's assassin, John Wilkes Booth. The
brothers had split on the issue of slavery and the Civil War.

century (Beethoven, who died in 1827, just made it into
the conventional Victorian–Gilded Age pantheon), Ingersoll actually enjoyed and supported the art of his own
time. He revered Whitman above all contemporary American poets and novelists, because his work gave a powerful,
distinctly American voice to humanism and the "religion
of the body" (another phrase Ingersoll used frequently).
Ingersoll turned most often to Shakespeare when he
wished to offer an emotional vision of human possibilities
unencumbered by gods and ghosts. He often described
Lear's soliloquy, on finding a place of refuge on the heath,
as "the greatest prayer that ever fell from human lips."[3]

> Poor naked wretches, wheresoe'er you are,
> That bide the pelting of this pitiless storm,
> How shall your unhoused heads, your unfed sides,
> Your looped and windowed raggedness, defend you
> From seasons such as these? Oh, I have ta'en
> Too little care of this. Take physic, pomp;
> Expose thyself to feel what wretches feel,
> That thou may'st shake the superflux to them,
> And show the heavens more just.

To Ingersoll, that prayer embodied his secularist creed.
He did not, however, regard acts of kindness and generosity, on an individual or a social level, as salvation-seeking
deeds of self-abnegation, self-sacrifice, or atonement for

sin mandated by religion but, on the contrary, as the surest way to attain a happy life for oneself.

Ingersoll delivered one of his most important and timely speeches citing Lear's soliloquy in New York, before a meeting of the American Secular Union on November 14, 1886. Only a month before, defendants in the socially polarizing Haymarket Square case—unquestionably the political trial of the century—had been sentenced to death. Tensions between rich and poor, always simmering beneath the surface of Gilded Age progress, had never been closer to the boiling point in the United States. On the evening of May 4, 1886, Chicago police arrived to disperse a peaceful assembly of workmen demonstrating on behalf of the eight-hour day, but a bomb (of unknown origin) was thrown, and police opened fire. Seven police officers and an unknown number of demonstrators and onlookers were killed, and eight of the protestors were indicted for murder.

Ingersoll himself had been asked to participate as counsel for the defense but declined because he felt that his antireligious reputation could only work against the defendants. He advised the defense team to "get a lawyer of national reputation who is a pillar of the church and who can cover these men with his conservative life and character."[4] Later, Ingersoll would plead for a commutation of the sentences with the Republican governor of Illinois, his old friend Richard Oglesby. The governor commuted three of the sentences to life imprisonment, but five of the defendants were executed. Oglesby's successor, John Peter Altgeld, a Democrat, would review the evidence and end his bright political career by pardoning those still in prison. It was against the backdrop of anti-labor passion generated by the recent trial that Ingersoll asked the Secular Union's upper-middle-class audience, "Is the world forever to remain as it was when Lear made his prayer? Is it ever to remain as it is now? I hope not. Are there always to be millions whose lips are white with famine? Is the withered palm to be always extended, imploring from the stony heart of respectable charity, alms? . . . Are the rich always to be divided from the poor,—not only in fact, but in feeling?"[5]

Ingersoll rejected the dictum, as widely preached in his time as it is now, that religion is the foundation of morality and that there can be no morality without religion. In Ingersoll's view, religion served only to provide supernatural explanations of and sanctions for conditions—whether decent or indecent—produced solely by the interaction between human beings and nature. The religion that had so recently been used to justify slavery, Ingersoll reminded his audiences, was every bit as powerful as the religious argument against slavery, and "thus sayeth the Lord" was used to isolate "the stony heart of respectable charity" from true exposure to "what wretches feel." Any morality that contradicted reason, nature, and the evidence supplied by this world, and relied instead on fantasies about another world presumed to lie beyond nature (and therefore beyond proof of any kind) would collapse as soon as fear of punishment was removed.

Ingersoll saw religion, not reason, as the cause of both the ascetic and traditional Christian idea that natural passions must be the enemy of virtuous moral conduct. He spoke frequently about this subject, particularly regarding the Pauline view of woman's body as a snare that diverted man from higher pursuits and the love of God.

Ingersoll's most biting commentary about Christian asceticism, however, appeared in an acerbic piece of literary criticism on Leo Tolstoy's embrace (if it can be called that) of chastity, poverty, and misogyny in "The Kreutzer Sonata," first published in 1889. Tolstoy's extremely long short story would not have been appropriate material for a popular lecture in the 1890s because few Americans, even the most educated, would have read it. In Tolstoy's jeremiad, the protagonist declares, "Sexual passion, no matter how it is arranged, is evil, a terrifying evil with which one has to struggle, and not encourage as we do now. The words of the Gospel about the one who looketh on a woman to lust after her hath committed adultery with her already refer not just to the wives of others, but precisely and especially to one's own."[6] To Ingersoll, this didactic writing—from the author of the masterpieces *War and Peace* and *Anna Karenina*—offered dismal evidence of the impact of religious fanaticism on even (or perhaps especially) the greatest minds; he considered Tolstoy's transition from writer to prophet of the joys of poverty and self-denial a cautionary example of religious extremism as the enemy of human achievement and progress.* In "The Kreutzer Sonata," Tolstoy had some nasty things to say about music as well as about sex and women as the enemies of morality in a work that advocates celibacy for both women and men—even within marriage. (It should be noted that the wife in "The Kreutzer Sonata" has an affair with an accomplished violinist, which naturally prompted Tolstoy to equate music with sexual debauchery.) Ingersoll observed that Tolstoy objected not to ordinary music "but to great music, the music that arouses the emotions, that apparently carries us beyond the limitations of life." Music, like sexual passion, generates powerful emotions,

---

*Tolstoy, born in 1828, was only five years older than Ingersoll. Raised, of course, in the Russian Orthodox Church, the writer experienced a deepening crisis of faith after completing *Anna Karenina* in 1877. Tolstoy's rejection of the flesh, wealth, and all sensual pleasures found its most famous expression in "The Kreutzer Sonata," which was held up by the official Tsarist censor because his advocacy of chastity even within marriage was actually a violation of the church's teachings. He was excommunicated by the Russian church in 1901.

and by the time Tolstoy wrote "The Kreutzer Sonata," he had become convinced that emotion is invariably at odds with duty and morality. Tolstoy and other religious ideologues had it exactly backward, Ingersoll argued. "Take emotions from the heart of man and the idea of obligation would be lost; right and wrong would lose their meaning. . . . We are subject to conditions, liable to disease, pain, and death. We are capable of ecstasy. Of these conditions, of these possibilities, the emotions are born." In a passage that displays the influence of both science (especially Darwinian evolution) and a love of earthly pleasures, Ingersoll wrote:

> We are conditioned beings; and if the conditions are changed, the result may be pain or death or greater joy. We can only live within certain degrees of heat. If the weather were a few degrees hotter or a few degrees colder, we could not exist. We need food and roof and raiment. Life and happiness depend on these conditions. We do not certainly know what is to happen, and consequently our hopes and fears are constantly active—that is to say, we are emotional beings. The generalization of Tolstoi, that emotion never goes hand in hand with duty, is almost the opposite of the truth. The idea of duty could not exist without emotion. Think of men and women without love, without desires, without passions!

Think of a world without art or music—a world
without beauty, without emotion.[7]

Ingersoll argued that unreasonable supernatural beliefs
were the result not of malice (though they were sometimes used maliciously by evil men) but of ignorance.
"Our fathers did they best they could," he acknowledged.
"They . . . thought that sacrifices and prayer, fasting and
weeping, would induce the Supernatural to give them
sunshine, rain and harvest—long life in this world and
eternal joy in another." This God was generous to his favorites and relentlessly punitive to his enemies, and man
was suspended between the two faces of God "like a
mouse between two paws."[8] Primitive humans should be
viewed with pity rather than censure, because they knew
nothing of the natural causes of disease; of earthquakes,
floods, and lightning; of physical or psychic pain and
could therefore do nothing but call upon the supernatural
to save them. But there was no excuse, in the state of evolution man had reached by the late nineteenth century,
for clinging to superstition as the only explanation for
and answer to problems that could be solved by human
effort. Here Ingersoll's disdain for myth fused with his
emotional and practical optimism. He looked at his own
time and saw discoverers, inventors, teachers, and scientists slowly taking the place of clerics. These develop-

ments led to his vision of a rich (in every sense of the word) future:

> The popes and priests and kings are gone,—the altars and the thrones have mingled with the dust,—the aristocracy of land and cloud have perished from the earth and air, and all the gods are dead. A new religion sheds its glory on mankind. It is the gospel of this world, the religion of the body, of the heart and brain, the evangel of health and joy. I see a world at peace, where labor reaps its true reward, a world without prisons, without workhouses, without asylums for the insane, a world on which the gibbet's shadow does not fall, a world where the poor girl, trying to win bread with the needle, the needle that has been called "the asp for the breast of the poor," is not driven to the desperate choice of crime or death, of suicide or shame. I see a world without the beggar's outstretched palm, the miser's stony stare, the piteous wail of want, the pallid face of crime, the livid lips of lies, the cruel eyes of scorn. I see a race without disease of flesh or brain, shapely and fair, the married harmony of form and use, and as I look life lengthens, fear dies, joy deepens, love intensifies. The world is free. This shall be.[9]

This level of optimism, which would begin its long decline on the blood-soaked battlefields of Europe only fifteen years after Ingersoll's death, is bound to seem archaic to anyone aware, as Ingersoll of course was not, of the real events of the twentieth century. Had he been able to see into the future, I think he would have concluded that Nazism and Stalinism had taken on all of the imperviousness to evidence of traditional religions and were therefore indistinguishable from any other form of blind faith.

This conjecture is based not only on my admiration for Ingersoll the freethinker but on his early recognition that science too was capable of veering into dangerous territory if its practitioners began to consider themselves infallible and therefore exempt from responding to the challenges of those outside their priesthood. Nowhere is this more evident than in Ingersoll's position on vivisection, which drew considerable criticism from those who considered themselves devotees of reason but clung to the irrational belief that science could and would be used only for good. Ingersoll warned of the ways in which science might be wrenched out of its proper position as the servant of humanity and used by powerful torturers as the servant of their omnipotent delusions—as nothing less than a new and evil form of faith. He described vivisection as "the Inquisition—the Hell—of Science" and physicians who would cut open conscious, living animals in order to "study" their pain as sadists who "would not hesitate to try experiments with men and women" simply to gratify curiosity.[10] Science was not a new God, and science—like religion—must be tested and judged by its results. Quoting distinguished surgeons, Ingersoll argued that surgical techniques had improved in his century not because of "the heartless tormentors of animals, but by the use of anaesthetics."[11]

Thus, vivisection was both cruel and scientifically worthless.* Even if the practice yielded some nugget of useful knowledge, though, Ingersoll insisted, "Brain without heart is far more dangerous than heart without brain" (see Appendix A).[12] To understand this man of the nineteenth century who anticipated the twentieth century, it is vital to realize that when he used the word "heart," Ingersoll did not mean antirational passion but the capacity for empathy that encompasses reason and emotion as allies rather than enemies and has emerged over ages of the evolution of the human brain.

---

*The deliberate infliction of pain on live animals in the name of science lasted well into the last quarter of the twentieth century. In his 2011 book *The Better Angels of Our Nature*, psychologist Steven Pinker recalls torturing a rat to death as a research assistant under the instructions of a Harvard professor. He described the act as "the single worst thing I have ever done."

VII
Death and Afterlife

You had better live well and die cursing than live badly
and die praying.
                    —RGI, "The Death Test"

In the summer of 1899, intensifying pain in his chest and
shortness of breath, caused by the heart disease he had
lived with for many years, forced Robert Ingersoll to end
his career as a lawyer and lecturer. His last two public appearances were concerned, in different ways, with the
rights of women. In early June, ten weeks before his death,
he made his impassioned statement, in a speech in Boston
before the American Free Religious Association, about
the need for women to possess the means to control their
own bodies and decide for themselves whether they wanted
to marry or become mothers. Later in the month, he
appeared in his last court case, in which he represented a
widow challenging her husband's will on grounds that he
had concealed the true value of his assets. The opposing

attorney expressed skepticism about whether a seventy-five-year-old man—the age of his client when he became engaged to his fifty-five-year-old future wife—could have truly been in love. (The stenographer's notes do not make clear exactly why the attorney thought the depth or shallowness of a man's love had any bearing on the validity of his will.) "I do not know what his experience is," Ingersoll said of the opposing counsel's cynicism about the possibility of love in old age, "but I hope no fate like that will ever overtake me."[1] Then Ingersoll retired from the public arena. He and his wife spent the last month of his life at the home, overlooking the Hudson River near Dobbs Ferry, New York, of their elder daughter, Eva, and her husband, railroad magnate Walston Brown. Mrs. Ingersoll's sister, Sue, and her husband, Clint Farrell, who would publish the definitive twelve-volume edition of Ingersoll's collected works, also lived with the Great Agnostic during his final weeks. The Ingersoll and Parker families were unusually close for in-laws; Mrs. Ingersoll's father had been a well-known freethinker in Peoria, and the family was related to Theodore Parker, a leading Transcendentalist, abolitionist, and reform-minded Unitarian minister in Boston during the two decades before the Civil War. But Robert had an extra reason for wanting the company of relatives while his own time was running out. He was well aware that after the deaths of nearly every important critic of religion, including Paine and Voltaire, the press and clergy circulated rumors that the "infidels" had either committed suicide in remorse for the unforgivable sin of denying the existence of God and the authority of his church (not that the clerics agreed on which church actually possessed divine authority) or had, at the last minute, renounced lifelong antireligious beliefs and begged God for forgiveness. Ingersoll wanted his wife, daughters, and in-laws to bear witness to his rejection of the supernatural even in the face of impending death.

Ingersoll died on July 21, 1899 (coincidentally, the day of Ernest Hemingway's birth). According to his obituary in the *New York World*, Ingersoll had spent the previous evening playing billiards with his brother-in-law. Having a cigar on the porch and looking toward the Hudson, he turned to Farrell and remarked, "This is a beautiful world." The next morning, after having breakfast with his family, he took a nap in his bedroom, with his wife watching over him. His sister-in-law came upstairs as he was about to dress for lunch and offered to bring up a tray so that he and Eva could eat together in the bedroom. "Oh no, I do not want to trouble you," was his last sentence. Sue Farrell made some joke, and Ingersoll laughed, closed his eyes, and died without further comments. The details are known because Eva Ingersoll and her sister gave the information to the press to counteract the already swirling rumors that Bob Ingersoll had either committed suicide in a fit of despair over his misspent life or called for a minister or a priest on his deathbed.*

Ingersoll would have particularly liked the headline over his obituary in the *Chicago Tribune*, "Ingersoll Dies Smiling." And he would probably have taken just as much pleasure in a paragraph in his *New York Times* obituary, which identified what was apparently a shocking character trait—no-strings generosity to his wife and children— in a nineteenth-century *paterfamilias*. "He earned great sums of money, both as a lecturer and a lawyer, but he let them go like water," the *Times* reported with an air of disapproval. "It was his habit to keep money in the house in an open drawer, to which any member of his family was free to go and take what he wanted."[2] One suspects, since all newspapers were wedded to the generic "he" at the time, that what really shocked the obituary writer was the fact that all of the members of Ingersoll's immediate family were women, and it was a "she," not a "he," who had been accorded such reckless access to cash. The obituary also noted that Ingersoll was "a constant student of Shakespeare" (presumably to his credit) but added that Shakespeare's works "occupied the place in his home where, in

* Seven years later, when the rumors had not ceased, Mrs. Ingersoll and her sister signed an affidavit attesting to the events of his last hours.

most of the homes in this country, the Bible rests" (presumably to his disgrace).

Ingersoll's funeral was simple, attended only by family and close friends, even as Eva Ingersoll received hundreds of telegrams and letters from famous and unknown men and women whose lives and thought had been changed by her husband's arguments. There was no music, although Ingersoll was a passionate lover of classical music and a generous donor to orchestral groups. A week after Ingersoll's death, the forty-member St. Nicholas Orchestra paid tribute to one of their major patrons with one of his favorite pieces of music, Siegfried's "Funeral March" from *Götterdämmerung*. When it was proposed that the music be played at his funeral, Eva Ingersoll said she could not bear to hear it while she was grieving so deeply. There was no eulogy, although the words Robert had spoken over his brother Ebon Clark's grave, when he died at age forty-seven in 1879, were read by a friend. Robert's tribute to his brother applied just as strongly to the Great Agnostic himself, who had used the lines in many of his speeches: "He believed that happiness is the only good, reason the only torch, justice the only worship, humanity the only religion, and love the only priest."[3] Robert had also set forth his own philosophy of peaceful death when he described his brother's final moments. "He who sleeps here, when dying, mistaking the approach of death for the return of health, whispered with his latest breath, 'I am better now.' Let us believe, in spite of doubts and dogmas, of fears and tears, that these dear words are true of all the countless dead."[4]

Ingersoll was cremated, according to his wishes, after the memorial service, and his wife kept his ashes on her bedroom mantel in their townhouse, in a vase with the inscription *L'urne garde la poussière, le coeur le souvenir* ("The urn guards the dust, the heart the memory"). At the time, cremation itself was an eloquent statement of Ingersoll's rejection of religion, since nearly all Christian denominations, as well as Judaism, not only frowned on but forbade the practice. In 1923, when Eva Ingersoll died, her ashes were mingled with her husband's. The urn was interred in 1932 by the family in Arlington National Cemetery, in what Ingersoll had often described as "the tongueless silence of the dreamless dust."[5] Coincidentally, the grave of William Jennings Bryan, who died shortly after the Scopes trial, is nearby.

Because Ingersoll died on a Friday, many ministers—especially in the cities where he had spoken most frequently—devoted their Sunday sermons to what they considered his blasphemous and unproductive life. Many of the divines shed crocodile tears at the distinguished career that Ingersoll might have had as a politician, a dip-

lomat, or a judge—if only he had not wasted his life trying
to destroy the religious foundation of society. One Presbyterian minister, quoted in the *Chicago Tribune*, predicted
that "it is as an opponent of Christianity that he will be
remembered . . . when he is remembered at all. Here his
work was destructive solely, without the desire to build."

The coverage of Ingersoll's death and its aftermath was
particularly extensive in Chicago, where Ingersoll first
rose to national prominence as an orator with his "Plumed
Knight" speech in 1876 and where he had returned many
times to preach the gospel of reason during his decades
as a resident of Washington and New York. A telling characteristic of the *Tribune* roundup of comments from the
clergy was that it consisted almost entirely of sermons by
Protestant ministers. There was no comment by a rabbi—
a half-century would pass before public figures began to
pay reflexive homage to "our Judaeo-Christian heritage"—
and only one sermon excerpt from a Catholic priest. Even
though Chicago was a city in the process of transformation by Catholic immigration from Italy and Slavic countries and by Jewish immigration from Russia and eastern
Europe, Protestant opinions were still considered the only
opinions that counted. The ministers alternated between
assertions that Ingersoll had had no effect at all on American religion (if this was so, one wonders why so many
divines devoted their sermons to speaking ill of the dead)

and anger at his successful efforts to lead misguided souls astray (especially, from the clerical perspective, the young, gullible, and poorly educated). The Reverend George A. Wallace, a Congregationalist minister, outdid the rest of the Chicago clergy with his claim that "all intelligent students of history know, Christianity and the church have been the authors and saviors of all the world's liberties, civil and religious."[6]

Notable for their absence from the public prints were the voices of prominent national Republican politicians whose campaigns had benefited so greatly from Ingersoll's political oratory. All Republican candidates for the presidency, beginning with Ulysses S. Grant, had been eager for the support of the crowds who gathered—in some instances, by the thousands—to hear Ingersoll speak on their behalf, but none of those still alive (including the sitting president, William McKinley) were willing to be associated with the nation's best-known heretic. Received opinion was also unanimous on another point: Republican presidents had been absolutely right to bar Ingersoll from any important appointive government job as a result of his agnosticism. President Rutherford B. Hayes rejected a proposal from Illinois Republicans that Ingersoll be named U.S. minister to Berlin in 1877. The *Times* commented approvingly in its obituary, "The suggestion that a dedicated and boasting unbeliever should be chosen

to represent a Christian country brought a storm of indignation." Indeed, the press itself had raised a storm about
Ingersoll's irreligion when his name was being bandied
about as a possible ambassador. Why, he could never use
the common German expression "Mein Gott!" According
to *The Washington Post*, Ingersoll was already employed in
the diplomatic corps as the "sleek, jolly plenipotentiary of
his Satanic Majesty to the United States of America."[7]

There were, of course, endless tributes to Ingersoll, but
most of them came from people already associated in
some way with religious unorthodoxy. Some of the most
powerful praise came from those on the left, like Eugene
V. Debs, who had disagreed with many of Ingersoll's political and economic opinions over the years. In the *Truth
Seeker* roundup of eulogies for the Great Agnostic, Debs
wrote:

> The name of Robert G. Ingersoll is written in the
> Pantheon of the world. More than any other man
> he destroyed religious superstition. Like an electric
> storm he purified the religious atmosphere. With rare
> courage and brilliant ability he applied himself to his
> tasks and won an immortality of gratitude and glory.
> He was the Shakespeare of oratory. . . . Ingersoll lived
> and died far in advance of his time. He fought nobly
> for the transformation of this world into a habitable

place, and long after the last echo of detraction will
be silence his name will be loved and honored and
his fame will shine resplendent, for his immortality
is fixed and glorious.[8]

Ingersoll's personal charm was so great (apparently, only
the *New York Times* could remain immune to the appeal of
a man who kept his cash in an unlocked drawer) that even
newspaper writers who felt obliged to condemn his antireligious views took care to separate the man from his
agnosticism. The *Chicago Tribune*, which dutifully reported
the universal disapproval of Ingersoll by the city's clergy,
concentrated on his personal qualities and speaking talents in the newspaper's first editorial commentary on his
death. The unsigned editorial noted, "To all Americans
who have heard and seen Robert G. Ingersoll on the stump
or the platform—and their name is legion—the news of
his departure from this world for another, which he had
no faith in, will be a surprise and a shock. They will feel
that they have lost an old familiar friend whose wit has
made them shriek with laughter and whose pathos has
unsealed the fountains of their tears."[9]

Despite the praise for Ingersoll's personal qualities in
much of the press commentary, the *Truth Seeker*, after an
exhaustive search, could find only two mainstream newspaper editorials with a good word for freethought itself.

In California, the *Stockton Daily Record* declared, "The age does not fully appreciate, but as the religion of superstition and impulse and passion gives way and the religion of intelligence, of love and justice is developed, he will be appreciated as a hero, and it is a grand compliment to the intelligence of the present age that he was not also a martyr."[10] This excerpt was unearthed by Frank Smith, the author of the most recent full-scale biography of Ingersoll, issued in 1990 by the freethought publisher Prometheus Books. It is a significant quotation because the small California paper was entirely accurate in its observation that someone who publicly espoused Ingersoll's views about religion would almost certainly have been martyred in a time and place that antedated the United States by only a century.

Ingersoll the crusading agnostic, and his influence on American thought and American religion, generated considerable heat in intellectual discourse for at least a quarter-century after his death. His message may have been troubling but was seldom derided by theologically liberal, intellectual Protestants—like the ministers he had debated—because most of them wished to accommodate Darwin's theory of evolution to their faith (and vice versa). The Unitarian minister and biblical scholar J. T. Sunderland, author of many erudite books that treated the Bible not as literally true but as divinely inspired, wrote in 1909 that Ingersoll had "pained the hearts not only of the ignorant, and the narrow, but of many of the most intelligent and broad-minded men and women" of his day and that his influence had lasted into the new century. Although Ingersoll had insulted believers with his irreverence, Sunderland praised him for having also "pricked the bubbles of many ecclesiastical and theological shams, hypocrisies, pretenses, make-believes" and being partly responsible, from the outside, for stimulating new thinking within religion.[11] This observation was strikingly similar to one made a century earlier, after the death of Thomas Paine, by the Unitarian William Bentley, pastor of the East Church in Salem, Massachusetts. Bentley, an Enlightenment polymath interested in everything from geology to American Indian culture, said of Paine: "He was indeed a wonderful man, & he was the first to see in what part every System was most vulnerable. Even in his attacks on Christianity he felt without knowing it, the greatest difficulties which rational Christians have felt."[12]

Fundamentalist Protestants had little to say about Ingersoll, although they remained deeply disturbed, in the decade after the Scopes trial, by the role of the freethought movement in seducing liberal Protestants into serious consideration of the theory of evolution. By then, however, fundamentalists were interested not in sparring with a ghost so far removed from their beliefs but in reversing the inroads that evolution was making in science classes and textbooks used in the growing number of American high schools.

The Roman Catholic Church—especially the scholarly Jesuits and Paulists—spoke out more forcefully against Ingersoll than it had during his lifetime. He was certainly blamed by Catholic bishops for having castigated, on every possible occasion, those who wished to obtain tax support for parochial schools. Although the church had given up (temporarily) on obtaining public revenue for Catholic education, its leaders were beginning to seize on the popular sentiment that linked patriotism with religion. In 1911, the Jesuit weekly publication *America* charged, "By destroying their belief in Christianity, Ingersoll did thousands of his fellow citizens an irreparable wrong and seriously imperiled his country's future, for a nation of unbelievers can never be a great or enduring nation."[13]

By the end of the First World War, when the blood-soaked Bolshevik Revolution ushered in the first Red Scare, Catholic immigrants were much more Americanized than they had been in Ingersoll's time, and the church had thrown in its lot with a nation that shared its strong opposition to communism and in which secularism itself could be identified as "un-American." The Reverend James M. Gillis, an influential Catholic scholar and editor of the

Catholic World, delivered a series of lectures in 1925 on secular thinkers, including Edward Gibbon, Paine, Voltaire, and Ingersoll. He described Ingersoll as a svengali for the uneducated and uncultured (although Gillis knew very well that the freethought movement appealed most strongly to the highly educated). "His fame, good or evil, persists as a tradition to the young," Gillis said, "as a memory to those of middle age. He is the nearest approach we Americans have had to Voltaire." Needless to say, the comparison to Voltaire was not intended as a compliment, though Ingersoll would surely have taken it as one.

It is understandable that Ingersoll remained more of a *bête noir* for Catholic than for Protestant intellectuals in the first three decades of the twentieth century. While mainstream Protestant denominations had dropped many of the rigid theological positions that Ingersoll had mocked so effectively, Catholic doctrine had not changed significantly. The American Catholic hierarchy was, if anything, even more theologically conservative after the First World War than it had been in the late nineteenth century. Papal infallibility, which had been adopted as Catholic dogma only in 1870, at the First Vatican Council, had always been treated as a particularly ridiculous idea by Ingersoll, whose fundamental argument against all religion was that

no individual or institution could claim divine authority.*
Such arguments made few inroads in the beliefs of the
nineteenth-century Catholic laity, with its large compo-
nent of poorly schooled immigrants. By the 1920s and
1930s, however, American Catholics were better educated
than they had been fifty years earlier. Ingersoll's old arguments against papal infallibility, newly advanced by others, were accessible to the growing number of well-off,
influential Catholics who were receiving a secular rather
than a Catholic religious education.†

Another explanation for the persistent Catholic animus toward "Ingersollism" was the increasing political
clout of Catholic voters and the growing willingness of
the hierarchy to campaign openly for laws that adhered
to church doctrine. The church had failed in its attempts
to gain tax support for parochial schools in the 1870s, but

---

*In a then-famous 1888 disputation with English cardinal Henry E. Man-
ning, Ingersoll wrote, "It may be sufficient to say that there is no crime that
man can commit that has not been committed by the vicars of Christ. . . .
Among [the popes] there were probably some good men. This would have happened even if the intention had been to get all bad men, for the reason that man
reaches perfection neither in good nor in evil; but if they were selected by
Christ himself, if they were selected by a church with a divine origin and under
divine guidance, then there is no way to account for the selection of a bad one.
If one hypocrite was duly elected pope one murderer, one strangler, one
starver—this demonstrates that all the popes were selected by men, and by men
only, and that the claim of divine guidance is born of zeal and uttered without
knowledge."

†The family of Joseph P. Kennedy, who sent his sons not to Catholic
schools but to the best secular prep schools and universities in the country, ex-
emplified this tendency.

it had much more success, in combination with the most conservative descendants of the Puritans, with new issues that arose in the twentieth century—most notably the availability of means of birth control that could be used by women. The arguments used by Ingersoll in favor of birth control before there were effective contraceptives were the same ones used by Margaret Sanger in her un-flagging attempts to make real twentieth-century birth control devices available to the poor as well as the rich. Translated into political action, the Catholic theological attack on birth control prevailed in Congress and many state legislatures in the decades between the wars, when new laws criminalizing the distribution and importation of contraceptives (including devices that, in contrast to petroleum jelly, actually worked) were added to the old Comstock laws.

Americans naturally had other, graver problems on their minds from the late 1920s through the mid-1940s, but the absence of an eloquent and widely recognized voice like Ingersoll's on behalf of the separation of church and state also helped marginalize a wide range of issues, from birth control to the teaching of evolution, until after the Second World War. In spite of the mistaken conclusion of many American intellectuals that fundamentalism was fin-ished, evolution actually lost ground in public school biol-ogy curriculums in the late 1920s and early 1930s. There was almost no discussion of this subject in the general news media for decades, although prominent scientists were appalled by the trend. In 1936, Oscar Riddle, a prominent biologist at the Station for Experimental Evolution in Cold Spring Harbor, New York, told the American Association for the Advancement of Science that high schools were teaching much less about evolution then they had in the first decade of the twentieth century.[14] But the proceedings of scientific meetings were not usually reported in mass-circulation newspapers. One of Ingersoll's greatest strengths had been his ability to reach beyond the scientific community, and there was no equally influential nonspecialist to alert Americans in the first half of the new century to the persistence of the most repressive forms of religion and their continuing battle to minimize the influence of scientific knowledge and understanding. (One compelling example of the largely undetected erosion of freethought advances in the late nineteenth and early twentieth centuries was a change in one of the standard high school science textbooks used throughout the nation for nearly four decades. The first edition of Truman Moon's *Biology for Beginners*, published in 1921, had a portrait of Darwin as the frontispiece. The second edition, published after the Scopes trial in 1926, replaced Darwin with a drawing of the human digestive tract. The 1920s also ushered in the downplaying of any connection between lower animals and human evolution. The E-word was censored and replaced in texts with euphemistic phrases like "changes over time." This cyclical antiscience drama returned in the first decade of the twenty-first century, with demands by the Texas State Board of Education—the second largest purchaser of school texts in the nation—for changes to minimize the subject of evolution in high school biology texts.)

By the 1920s, the last generation of Americans who came of age while Ingersoll was in his prime were growing old, but to freethinkers, the issues raised by the Great Agnostic were far from settled. "A great many people contend that we now enjoy in this country as much liberty (or toleration) as is good for us," essayist Michael Monahan, born in 1865, wrote. "To aim at the full measure which Colonel Ingersoll advocated is, in the opinion of these people, to advance the standard of Anarchy. By this reasoning a man who is only half or three-quarters well is better off than one in perfect health." Monahan pointed out the tendency of contemporary religious leaders to dismiss Ingersoll as one who wasted his life taking on theological straw-men, "fighting battles that had been thoroughly fought out before his day." (This position would also be taken by the few secular scholars who revisited Ingersoll in the 1960s and 1970s.) Monahan was one of the few cultural commentators of any generation to agree with my view that Ingersoll belongs to the ranks of classical liberals rather than of social Darwinists and that he was a true philosophical descendant of Thomas Paine. "Ingersoll was no mere echo and imitator of the great liberals who preceded him," Monahan asserted. ". . . He was the best-equipped, most formidable and persistent advocate of the liberal principal which this country, at least, has ever known; and it is extremely doubtful if his equal as a popular propagandist was to be found anywhere."[15] What were those liberal principles? Ingersoll believed "that everyone was entitled to comfort, well-being, happiness in this world. . . . He regarded pauperism not as a proof of the special favor of God, but as an indictment of man. . . . He pleaded for the abolition of the death penalty, that relic of savagery. . . . His great heart went out in sympathy to everything that suffers—to the dumb animals, beaten and overladen; to the feathered victims of caprice and cruelty."*

In spite of the disappearance of "Ingersollism" as a controversial topic in the public prints around 1930, his memory remains a sensitive topic in parts of the country where agnosticism, atheism, secularism, and freethought are still

---

* During the Gilded Age, the demand for feathers, especially ostrich plumes, to decorate ladies' hats was so great that various species were threatened. Along with the anti-vivisection movement, outrage at the destruction of birds for millinery was one of the earliest animal rights campaigns.

189

dirty words. In 2001, I visited Dowagiac, Michigan, the town that welcomed Ingersoll in 1893 to speak at the opening of a grand theater named in honor of the area's leading employer and citizen, the freethinking Philo D. Beckwith. In one of the fits of destructive urban renewal that destroyed old buildings across the country in the 1960s, the Beckwith Theater, with its busts of famous freethinkers, was razed to make way for an office building. Some of the busts were rescued from the wrecking ball by local preservationists, while others were pulverized. I tracked down Beethoven and Paine on the grounds of a local college, but Ingersoll was nowhere to be found— or so I was told. When I asked several town officials about the whereabouts of Ingersoll's head, they assured me it had not been seen since the day in 1968 when the historic building was destroyed in the interest of progress. This story turned out to be, if one takes a charitable viewpoint, a manifestation of the local burghers' ignorance of their town history. If one adheres to a less charitable interpretation, they were telling a deliberate lie. The Ingersoll bust had been rescued from the dust on that day in 1968 by two local freethinkers, Jack Ruple and Joseph Spadefore, who, at age ninety-one, still lived in Dowagiac on what was once the town's main shopping street. When I finally tracked him down for an interview, Spadefore— referring familiarly to Ingersoll as "Bob"—laughed at the idea that local businessmen and civic leaders might think that the Ingersoll bust was no more. Since 1968, he told me, Ingersoll's bronze head had been "planted in the ground, like those flamingos some people have on their lawns, at the side of Jack Ruple's driveway. We didn't have anywhere else to put it." Spadefore had attempted many times to persuade the city council to preserve the bust and display it prominently as a memento of the town's free-thought history. "I was just considered a crazy old man," he said. "I'm sure a lot of people around here still think that old Bob deserved to be reduced to smithereens in vengeance by an angry God, so they just told you that's what happened."

In 2001, the bust was salvaged again by author and freethinking minister Roger E. Greeley, who drove the sculpture across the country to its present home at the Ingersoll Birthplace Museum in Dresden. "I'm sure those secular humanists in New York will take good care of Bob," Spadefore said, "but as for me, I'd like to walk past a statue of him right here in Dowagiac." Spadefore had lived in Dowagiac for most of his adult life, and as a young man, he read the speech Ingersoll delivered about Beck-with in the collected works published in 1900. "Bob's writings were still in the local library then," Spadefore re-called, "and I read all twelve volumes of them. Imagine, this stuff is still controversial."

Afterword
A Letter to the "New" Atheists

There is no such thing as a new atheist. You know this, of course, and are usually careful to give ample credit to your predecessors. They made you possible, by waging the battle for reason and freedom of conscience at considerable risk to their own lives and liberty—whether by speaking out against the received opinion of their times or by the scientific investigation that led to a natural rather than a supernatural explanation of how our entire universe, including human beings, came to be. The names of Copernicus, Galileo, Giordano Bruno, Spinoza, Voltaire, Paine, Humboldt, and, of course, Darwin are frequently on your lips and in your books, as well they should be. Upon the shoulders of these giants rest the efforts of all whose aim is to make gentle the life of this world rather than to seek paradise in some hidden world beyond nature. So why is Robert Green Ingersoll usually absent from your honor roll?

I would not expect you to mention Ingersoll if you were promoting the idea that America is, after all, a Christian nation founded by Christians who intended to establish a Christian government. But you are all dedicated to the advancement of the same secular values that Ingersoll advocated in a much more religious era. Had there been no Ingersoll to continue Paine's work of laying the foundation for future, unassured, yet eminently possible ages of American reason, there would be a much smaller audience today not only for you but for liberal religious believers who, instead of caving in to right-wing myths about America having been established as a quasi-theocracy, have fought and are still fighting efforts to impose parochial religious dogma on public policy.

Sometimes I suspect that Ingersoll's nineteenth-century designation as the Great Agnostic—not the Great Atheist—is the real reason why so many prominent twenty-first century atheists have placed scant emphasis on his role in American history. A neutral descriptive term in Europe today, *atheist* remains a pejorative to many religious Americans. I would not be surprised if some of you imagine that Ingersoll was trying to fudge his real beliefs to attain greater public respectability, as some American agnostics do today. Not so. When offered the opportunity many times by journalists to distinguish his agnosticism from atheism, Ingersoll never took the bait and always replied that there was no difference between the two. Whether one called oneself an atheist or an agnostic, Ingersoll emphasized, it was impossible to "prove" a negative such as the nonexistence of God. Ingersoll would cheerfully accept being called an atheist by those who considered the word a worse epithet than *agnostic*. That ought to be good enough for any outspoken atheist today— especially since there are still so many Americans who embrace the misapprehension that all atheists claim to "know" that God does not exist. Such people will often state, with an air of moral superiority, that they are agnostics because they do not subscribe to "atheist fundamentalism." They do not understand that fundamentalism (if what is meant by fundamentalism is belief in the literal truth and divine authorship of ancient books) has nothing to do with atheism, and that the atheist, like the self-described agnostic, regards proofs of the existence of God in the same light that David Hume regarded proofs of miracles. With Hume, the atheist says, "No testimony is sufficient to establish a miracle, unless the testimony be of such a kind, that its falsehood would be more miraculous than the fact which it endeavours to establish."

Many of you (including those, like Richard Dawkins and

the late Christopher Hitchens, born and educated in England) have devoted a good deal of your proselytizing energy to the United States because this is the only developed country whose inhabitants still cling, in significant numbers, to the idea that their nation and their way of life was ordained by God. What these particular Americans mean by God is not some vague, overarching providence but a particular god who shed his divinity to walk the earth some two thousand years ago and died on a cross to redeem us (including you heretics) from the original sin committed in the Garden of Eden. And so, you rightly emphasize one of the great paradoxes of American history—the founding of the world's first secular government at a time when the American people were even more overwhelmingly Christian, specifically Protestant, than they are today. In the pantheon of American freethinkers, you rarely fail to mention, at some point, the role played in the establishment of our secular government by the many Enlightenment rationalists among the founders. You always single out Benjamin Franklin, Thomas Jefferson, and James Madison not only as the founders of the new nation but also as the progenitors of an American tradition that enshrines no religion—unless intellectual liberty is considered religion. Again I ask: Where is Ingersoll in your accounts of subsequent chapters in the story of American secularism?

The nineteenth-century media identification of Ingersoll with agnosticism is not the only reason for his obscure standing in the atheist pantheon today. Another explanation can be traced to the criticism of Ingersoll, both before and after his death, on grounds that he was not an "original thinker" but merely a synthesizer and popularizer of other people's ideas. He was certainly not a scientist, a philosopher, or a historian recognized by scholarly institutions. But that was precisely Ingersoll's strength: He believed that reason was available to and attainable by the many and not restricted to the educated few. He saw the writings of Shakespeare, Spinoza, Voltaire, Paine, Jefferson, and Humboldt as comprehensible to all; a degree in the natural sciences, philosophy, or literature was not required to enter Ingersoll's house of reason. This is hardly a moot argument today, given that a continuing feature of our political culture is the denigration of reason itself as an "ivory tower" phenomenon that could not possibly be important to anyone but a professor in his or her study. There is no "merely" about Ingersoll's role as a popularizer of freethought, because when the cause is reason itself, and the capacity of reason to alter human lives for the better, nothing can be accomplished without widespread dissemination among members of the public from diverse educational backgrounds and social classes. Ingersoll left a priceless legacy not only to committed atheists but to secularists who—like many of the American founders—

may believe in some form of Providence but are convinced that any universal spirit has left it up to humans to solve earthly problems through our own reason.

Ingersoll labored mightily to cut through the layers of religious treacle that separated Americans of his country's second century, for all their more advanced technology, from the Enlightenment rationalists who wrote a founding document beginning with the words "We the People" rather than with acknowledgment of gratitude and servitude to some divinity. He was the missing link between the revolutionary generation and millions of late nineteenth-century Americans, whether born in the New World or the Old, who had forgotten or never knew that their nation was built on the premise of human, not divine, authority.

None of this history is far removed from the task of twenty-first-century atheists and secularists. The audience for the new-old atheists includes a good many Americans in their thirties whose great-grandparents might well have heard Ingersoll invite them to join him and other freethinkers in "laying the foundations of the grand temple of the future—not the temple of all the gods, but of all the people." My own grandfather, born in 1872, attended many of Ingersoll's lectures. Does his interest in one of the two greatest freethinkers in American history have anything to do with the fact that I, and my two nieces in their twenties, are atheists? I cannot be certain, but I do know that doubt, like faith, is generally transmitted over generations; there is rarely a single moment, the equivalent of Saul falling off his horse on the road to Damascus, in which people slap their heads and say, "Eureka, Christ is the Lord!" or "Eureka, there is no all-powerful, loving God!" Faith and reason are always in the air we breathe: Ingersoll was one of the grand doubters who labored to clear the environment of poisonous certitude for future generations.

First, he explained the true meaning and value of science as a system of inquiry whose tentative conclusions were always open to modification by new evidence. He explained this in a more understandable fashion than any scientist, even the brilliant popularizer Thomas Henry Huxley, did at the time and in more lucid fashion than any scientist, with the possible exception of Dawkins, is doing right now. It may even have been better that Ingersoll was not a scientist, because the notion that there is some vast divide between the "mysteries" of science and ordinary human intelligence, that science and religion or, for that matter, science and the humanities, must occupy "separate magisteria" was one of the most pernicious intellectual fashions of the second half of the twentieth century. In Ingersoll's time, specialization had not yet triumphed, and the idea that one had to be a scientist to understand the scientific method, or to talk about it, was considered highly suspect by most Americans. Science is not a mystery,

Ingersoll told his audiences, and scientists are not priests, bishops, or popes. The latter half of the proposition was arguably as important as the former, because some in his generation were led by their passion for science into pseudosciences that took on some of the characteristics of religious orthodoxy. These late nineteenth-century scientific-*seeming* byways ranged from the prevailing social Darwinism of many Gilded Age intellectuals and business leaders to the arrogance of the vivisectionists, whose claims that they had a perfect right to torture lower animals in the name of science were not all that far removed from the biblical assertion that God had created man with dominion over the birds of the air and the beasts of the field.

Second, Ingersoll made the connection between repressive religion and everyday burdens and injustices as no one had before him. The Enlightenment rationalists, especially Paine and Voltaire, understood and excoriated the role of religion, coupled with state power, in large issues that included slavery, torture, and capital punishment. Ingersoll spoke out on the same issues but moved farther and deeper into the most intimate injustices sanctioned by society. As far as he was concerned, there were no social injustices in which religion did not play a major role—from the prevalent belief, well into the nineteenth century, that God had created the poor for a reason and that only those who could pay deserved to be educated, to the religiously based laws and customs that sanctioned marital violence, deemed it a moral disgrace for a woman to leave her husband for any reason, and denied women access to education and the means of making a living. Debtors' prisons, cruelty to children and animals, inhumane treatment both of the insane and of criminals: All were justified by biblical precepts that formed the original basis for mistreatment of the powerless by the powerful. Ingersoll did not live to see twentieth-century totalitarianism, but there is little doubt, given his contempt for the idea that "tooth and claw" should be the rule for man in a state of civilization, that he would have had equal contempt for secular ideologies that took on the anti-rational, anti-evidentiary characteristics of orthodox theology.

Finally, Ingersoll's primary civic aim was the restoration of the historical memory of a founding generation that had explicitly rejected theocracy as the basis for a national government. His American patriotism was inseparable from his valorization of the separation of church and state. To him, the glory of the founding generation was that it did *not* establish a Christian nation. There is no establishment figure who says anything of the kind in America today. Even though Ingersoll was denied the opportunity for public office because of his antireligious beliefs, he was nevertheless very much a part of the social and political establishment. Yet he placed his principles, and his determination that Americans not forget the secular side of their own history, above his considerable political ambitions—something that no aspirant to high office has been willing to do in the United States since ... well, since Ingersoll himself. There ought to be some sort of Atheist Hall of Fame—it would not be large—for those who refuse to engage in religious hypocrisy to further their political ambitions.

Ingersoll belongs there. Eliminate a few Victorianisms, and everything he had to say in his time is just as relevant to a nation in which religious censors are still trying to eliminate the very idea of the separation of church and state from school history texts and a world in which radical Islamist theocrats still want blasphemers to die for their "crimes."

Like atheists of this generation, Ingersoll was constantly charged by his religiously orthodox contemporaries with the crime of attempting to destroy comforting beliefs in divine guidance while replacing them with nothing, leaving forlorn men and women to roam the earth in a state of fear because nothing can make this life worthwhile in the absence of faith in an afterlife. To this Ingersoll replied, as atheists do today, that nothing in a putative eternity could possibly justify suffering in this world and that the reduction of suffering in one, finite lifetime is a high goal for any human being. Given the existence of evils long attributed to gods, Ingersoll saw no reason for humans to be intimidated by the idea that they were on their own in the task of building a better future. "Man through his intelligence must protect himself," Ingersoll said equably. "He gets no help from any other world." What would be left when the men and women banished the ghosts of gods who destroyed or ennobled humans on the basis of divine whim? "The world remains," Ingersoll replied, "with . . . homes and firesides, where grow and bloom the virtues of our race. . . . Let the ghosts go. We will worship them no more. Let them cover their eyeless sockets with their fleshless hands and fade forever from the imaginations of men."

You "new" atheists should consider it your special duty and privilege to work tenaciously for the restoration of the memory of this old American freethinker. You owe him. So does every American, religious or nonreligious, who enjoys and takes for granted that liberty of conscience is meant for thee as well as for me—the greatest secular idea of all.

Appendix A
Vivisection

Vivisection is the Inquisition—the Hell—of Science. All the cruelty which the human—or rather the inhuman—heart is capable of inflicting, is in this one word. Below this there is no depth. This word lies like a coiled serpent at the bottom of the abyss.

We can excuse, in part, the crimes of passion. We take into consideration the fact that man is liable to be caught by the whirlwind, and that from a brain on fire the soul rushes to a crime. But what excuse can ingenuity form for a man who deliberately—with an unaccelerated pulse—with the calmness of John Calvin at the murder of Servetus—seeks, with curious and cunning knives, in the living, quivering flesh of a dog, for all the throbbing nerves of pain? The wretches who commit these infamous crimes pretend that they are working for the good of man; that they are actuated by philanthropy; and that their pity for the sufferings of the human race drives out all pity for the animals they slowly torture to death. But those who are incapable of pitying animals are, as a matter of fact, incapable of pitying men. A physician who would cut a living rabbit in pieces—laying bare the nerves, denuding them with knives, pulling them out with forceps—would not hesitate to try experiments with men and women for the gratification of his curiosity.

To settle some theory, he would trifle with the life of any patient in his power. By the same reasoning he will justify the vivisection of animals and patients. He will say that it is better that a few animals should suffer than that one human being should die; and that it is far better that one patient should die, if through the sacrifice of that one, several may be saved.

Brain without heart is far more dangerous than heart without brain.

Have these scientific assassins discovered anything of value? They may have settled some disputes as to the action of some organ, but have they added to the useful knowledge of the race?

It is not necessary for a man to be a specialist in order to have and express his opinion as to the right or wrong of vivisection. It is not necessary to be a scientist or a naturalist to detest cruelty and love mercy. Above all the discoveries of the thinkers, above all the inventions of the ingenious, above all the victories won on fields of intellectual conflict, rise human sympathy and a sense of justice.

I know that good for the human race can never be accomplished by torture. I also know that all that has been ascertained by vivisection could have been done by the dissection of the dead. I know that all the torture has been useless. All the agony inflicted has simply hardened the hearts of the criminals, without enlightening their minds.

It may be that the human race might be physically improved if all the sickly and deformed babes were killed, and if all the paupers, liars, drunkards, thieves, villains, and vivisectionists were murdered. All this might, in a few ages, result in the production of a generation of physically perfect men and women; but what would such beings be worth,—men and women healthy and heartless, muscular and cruel—that is to say, intelligent wild beasts?

Never can I be the friend of one who vivisects his fellow-creatures. I do not wish to touch his hand.

When the angel of pity is driven from the heart; when the fountain of tears is dry,—the soul becomes a serpent crawling in the dust of the desert.

—Robert Ingersoll to Philip G. Peabody, May 27, 1890

Appendix B
Robert Ingersoll's Eulogy for Walt Whitman, March 30, 1892

My friends: Again, we, in the mystery of Life, are brought face to face with the mystery of Death. A great man, a great American, the most eminent citizen of this Republic, lies dead before us, and we have met to pay a tribute to his greatness and his worth.

I know he needs no words of mine. His fame is secure. He laid the foundations of it deep in the human heart and brain. He was, above all I have known, the poet of humanity, of sympathy. He was so great that he rose above the greatest that he met without arrogance, and so great that he stooped to the lowest without conscious condescension. He never claimed to be lower or greater than any of the sons of men.

He came into our generation a free, untrammeled

spirit, with sympathy for all. His arm was beneath the form of the sick. He sympathized with the imprisoned and despised, and even on the brow of crime he was great enough to place the kiss of human sympathy.

One of the greatest lines in our literature is his, and the line is great enough to do honor to the greatest genius that has ever lived. He said, speaking of an outcast: "Not till the sun excludes you do I exclude you."

His charity was wide as the sky, and wherever there was human suffering, human misfortune, the sympathy of Whitman bent above it as the firmament bends above the earth.

He was built on a broad and splendid plane—ample, without appearing to have limitations—passing easily for a brother of mountains and seas and constellations; caring nothing for the little maps and charts with which timid pilots hug the shore, but giving himself freely with reck-lessness of genius to winds and waves and tides; caring for nothing as long as the stars were above him. He walked among men, among writers, among verbal varnishers and veneerers, among literary milliners and tailors, with the unconscious majesty of an antique god.

He was the poet of that divine democracy which gives equal rights to all the sons and daughters of men. He ut-tered the great American voice; uttered a song worthy of the great Republic. No man ever said more for the rights of humanity, more in favor of real democracy, of real justice. He neither scorned nor cringed, was neither tyrant nor slave. He asked only to stand the equal of his fellows beneath the great flag of nature, the blue and stars.

He was the poet of Life. It was a joy simply to breathe. He loved the clouds; he enjoyed the breath of morning, the twilight, the wind, the winding streams. He loved to look at the sea when the waves burst into whitecaps of joy. He loved the fields, the hills; he was acquainted with the trees, with birds, with all the beautiful objects of the earth. He not only saw these objects, but understood their meaning, and he used them that he might exhibit his heart to his fellow-men.

He was the poet of Love. He was not ashamed of that divine passion that has built every home in the world; that divine passion that has painted every picture and given us every real work of art; that divine passion that has made the world worth living in and has given some value to human life.

He was the poet of the natural, and taught men not to be ashamed of what is natural. He was not only the poet of democracy, not only the poet of the great Republic, but he was the poet of the human race. He was not confined to the limits of this country, but his sympathy went out over the seas to all the nations of the earth.

He stretched out his hand, and he felt himself the equal

of all kings and all princes, and the brother of all men, no matter how high, no matter how low.

He has uttered more supreme words than any writer of our century, possibly of almost any other. He was, above all things, a man, and above genius, above all the snow-capped peaks of intelligence, above all art, rises the true man. Greater than all is the true man, and he walked among his fellow-men as such.

He was the poet of Death. He accepted all life and all death, and he justified all. He had the courage to meet all, and was great enough and splendid enough to harmonize all and to accept all there is of life as a divine melody . . .

He was absolutely true to himself. He had frankness and courage, and he was as candid as light. He was willing that all the sons of men should be absolutely acquainted with his heart and brain. He had nothing to conceal. Frank, candid, pure, serene, noble, and yet for years he was maligned and slandered, simply because he had the candor of nature. He will be understood yet, and that for which he was condemned—his frankness, his candor—will add to the glory and greatness of his fame.

He wrote a liturgy for mankind; he wrote a great and splendid psalm of life, and he gave to us the gospel of humanity—the greatest gospel that can be preached.

He was not afraid to live, not afraid to die. For many years he and death were near neighbors. He was always willing and ready to meet and greet this king called death, and for many months he sat in the deepening twilight waiting for the night, waiting for the light.

He never lost his hope. When the mists filled the valleys, he looked upon the mountain tops, and when the mountains in darkness disappeared, he fixed his gaze upon the stars.

In his brain were blessed memories of the day, and in his heart were mingled the dawn and dusk of life.

He was not afraid; he was cheerful every moment. The laughing nymphs of day did not desert him. They remained that they might clasp the hands and greet with smiles the veiled and silent sisters of the night. And when they did come, Walt Whitman stretched his hand to them. On one side were the nymphs of the day, and on the other the silent sisters of the night, and so, hand in hand, between smiles and tears, he reached his journey's end.

From the frontier of life, from the western wave-kissed shore, he sent us messages of content and hope, and these messages seem now like strains of music blown by the "Mystic Trumpeter" from Death's pale realm.

To-day we give back to Mother Nature, to her clasp and kiss, one of the bravest, sweetest souls that ever lived in human clay.

Charitable as the air and generous as Nature, he was

negligent of all except to do and say what he believed he should do and say.

And I to-day thank him, not only for you but for myself, for all the brave words he has uttered. I thank him for all the great and splendid words he has said in favor of liberty, in favor of man and woman, in favor of motherhood, in favor of fathers, in favor of children, and I thank him for the brave words he has said of death.

He has lived, he has died, and death is less terrible than it was before. Thousands and millions will walk down into the "dark valley of the shadow" holding Walt Whitman by the hand. Long after we are dead the brave words he has spoken will sound like trumpets to the dying.

And so I lay this little wreath upon this great man's tomb. I loved him living, and I love him still.

Notes

INTRODUCTION

1. Robert Green Ingersoll (hereafter RGI), "Individuality," *The Works of Robert Ingersoll* (New York, 1900), vol. 1, p. 201.
2. RGI, "Centennial Oration," *Works*, vol. 9, p. 74.
3. Ibid.
4. Ibid., p. 93.
5. In C. H. Cramer, *Royal Bob: The Life of Robert G. Ingersoll* (New York, 1952), p. 102.
6. RGI, "The Gods," *Works*, vol. 1, p. 88.
7. RGI, *Works*, vol. 8, p. 191.
8. In Roger E. Greeley, *Ingersoll: Immortal Infidel* (Buffalo, NY, 1977), p. 160.
9. *Mason City Republican*, June 11, 1885, cited in Cramer, *Royal Bob*, p. 218.
10. RGI, "Some Mistakes of Moses," *Works*, vol. 2, pp. 130–131.
11. RGI, *Works*, vol. 8, p. 393.
12. Ibid., pp. 394–395.
13. *Philadelphia Times*, September 25, 1885.

14. Theodore Roosevelt, *Gouverneur Morris* (Oyster Bay, NY, 1975), p. 174.
15. RGI to John Ingersoll, August 1, 1891, quoted in Orvin Larson, *American Infidel: Robert G. Ingersoll* (New York, 1962), p. 195.
16. Frederick Lewis Allen, *Only Yesterday* (New York, 1959), pp. 48–49.
17. *New York Times*, July 22, 1899.
18. Edgar W. Howe, *The Atchison-Daily Globe*, July 21, 1899, quoted in Roger Greeley, *Ingersoll: Immortal Infidel*, p. 158.

CHAPTER I
The Making of an Iconoclast

1. Edward G. Smith, *The Life & Reminiscences of Robert Green Ingersoll* (New York, 1904), cited in C. H. Cramer, *Royal Bob*, p. 20.
2. Cameron Rogers, *Colonel Bob Ingersoll: A Biographical Narrative of the Great American Orator and Agnostic* (New York, 1927), p. 2.
3. Larson, *American Infidel*, p. 15.
4. RGI, "Why I Am an Agnostic," *Works*, vol. 4, p. 27.
5. Ibid., p. 25.
6. Ibid, p. 24.
7. RGI, letter to *Utica Herald*, November 5, 1877, in Frank Smith, *Robert G. Ingersoll: A Life* (Buffalo, NY, 1990), p. 19.
8. RGI, "On the Liberty of Man, Woman, and Child," *Works*, vol. 1, pp. 377–379.
9. RGI, *Works*, vol. 12, p. 172.
10. Ibid., pp. 172–173.
11. Quoted in Larson, *American Infidel*, p. 46.
12. RGI to Ebon Clark Ingersoll, April 24, 1862, Ingersoll Papers, Illinois State Historical Library.
13. Affidavit by Lt. Col. Meek, *Truth Seeker*, August 9, 1924, cited in Cramer, *Royal Bob*, p. 54.
14. RGI, "An Address to the Colored People," *Works*, vol. 9, p. 7.
15. Ibid., p. 6.
16. RGI, *Works*, vol. 5, p. 302.
17. Ibid., pp. 302–303.

CHAPTER II

The Political Insider and the Religious Outsider

1. RGI, "The Gods," *Works*, vol. 1, p. 9.
2. RGI, "Centennial Oration," *Works*, vol. 9, p. 55.
3. *Chicago Times*, June 16, 1876.
4. *A History and Criticism of American Public Address*, ed. William Norwood Brigance (New York, 1943), pp. 370–371.
5. Mark Twain, "The Chicago G.A.R. Festival," in *Autobiography of Mark Twain*, ed. Harriet Elinor Smith (Berkeley, CA, 2011), vol. 1, p. 69.
6. Abraham Lincoln, *The Collected Works of Abraham Lincoln* (New Brunswick, NJ, 1953), vol. 5, pp. 419–420.
7. RGI to Clint Farrell, November 9, 1884.
8. *Commonwealth*, Topeka, Kansas, November 21, 1884.
9. *New York Tribune*, April 4, 1885.
10. *New York Sun*, August 26, 1876.
11. Harry Thurston Peck, *"What Is Good English?" and Other Essays* (New York, 1899), p. 236.
12. *New York Times*, May 24, 1880.
13. In George E. MacDonald, *Fifty Years of Freethought* (New York, 1929), vol. 2, pp. 123–124.
14. Sidney Warren, *American Freethought, 1860–1914* (New York, 1943), pp. 94–95.
15. RGI, "A Tribute to Philo D. Beckwith," *Works*, vol. 12, pp. 482–483.
16. RGI, "A Tribute to Walt Whitman," *Works*, vol. 12, p. 476.
17. *Dowagiac Times*, January 19, 1893.

CHAPTER III

Champion of Science

1. RGI, "Superstition," *Works*, vol. 4, pp. 325–326.
2. *New York Times*, September 23, 1876.
3. Ibid.
4. RGI, "The Liberty of Man, Woman, and Child," *Works*, vol. 1, pp. 392–395.

5. "Apostate's Creed," *Christian Worker's Magazine*, in Cramer, *Royal Bob*, p. 128.
6. RGI, "The Ghosts," *Works*, vol. 1, p. 288.
7. RGI, "The Gods," *Works*, vol. 1, pp. 44–45.
8. RGI, "Orthodoxy," *Works*, vol. 2, p. 259.
9. Herman E. Kittredge, *Ingersoll: A Biographical Appreciation* (New York, 1911).
10. Hamlin Garland, *Roadside Meetings* (New York, 1930), p. 44.
11. Ibid., p. 47.
12. "Interview with Col. Robert Ingersoll," *Truth Seeker*, September 5, 1885.
13. Ibid.
14. RGI, "A Tribute to Henry Ward Beecher," *Works*, vol. 12, pp. 419, 423–424.
15. *Boston Investigator*, July 20, 1880.

CHAPTER IV
The Humanistic Freethinker

1. *Proceedings of the National Convention to Secure the Religious Amendment of the Constitution of the United States, Held in Cincinnati, January 31 and February 1, 1872* (Philadelphia, 1872), pp. viii–x, in Morton Borden, *Jews, Turks, and Infidels* (Chapel Hill, NC, 1984), p. 69.
2. *Chicago Tribune*, August 27, 1900, in Cramer, *Royal Bob*, p. 232.
3. RGI, "A Lay Sermon," *Works*, vol. 4, p. 223.
4. RGI, "Some Interrogation Points," *Works*, vol. 11, pp. 185–186.
5. RGI, "Eight Hours Must Come," *Works*, vol. 11, pp. 451–453.
6. Charles Darwin, *The Descent of Man*, Modern Library edition combined with *On the Origin of Species* (New York, 1948), pp. 500–501.
7. Henry Ward Beecher, "Communism Denounced," *New York Times*, July 30, 1877.
8. RGI, "Civil Rights," *Works*, vol. 11, p. 2.
9. *National Republican*, Washington, DC, October 17, 1883.
10. "Speech to the 'Opening Convention of the National Woman Suffrage Association, January 19 and 20, 1869,'" Elizabeth Cady Stanton Papers, Library of Congress, Washington, DC.

11. RGI, "Eight Hours Must Come," p. 487.
12. RGI, "Should the Chinese Be Excluded?" *North American Review*, July 1893.
13. Ibid.
14. Ibid.
15. RGI, "What Is Religion?" *Works*, vol. 4, p. 505.
16. RGI, Preface to Helen Hamilton Gardener, *Men, Women, and Gods*, available at http://www.gutenberg.org/ebooks30207.
17. "Woman's Right to Divorce," *New York World*, 1988, *Works*, vol. 8, p. 385.
18. Ingersoll, "Preface to 'For Her Daily Bread,'" *Works*, vol. 12, p. 49.
19. RGI, Preface, *Men, Women, and Gods*.
20. RGI, "The Liberty of Man, Woman, and Child," *Works*, vol. 1, p. 371.
21. "Working Girls," *New York World*, December 2, 1888.
22. Ibid.
23. RGI, "Secular Thought," August 25, 1898, *Works*, vol. 8, p. 391.
24. RGI, "Secularism," *Works*, vol. 11, p. 405.
25. Ibid., p. 406.
26. Herbert Spencer, *Social Statics* (New York, 1864), p. 415.

CHAPTER V

Church and State

1. RGI, "Address to the Jury in the Trial of C. B. Reynolds," *Works*, vol. 11, p. 109.
2. Ibid., p. 108.
3. Ibid., p. 117.
4. *New York Times*, May 20, 1887.
5. D. McAllister, "Testimonies to the Religious Defect of the Constitution" (Philadelphia, 1874), quoted in Borden, *Jews, Turks, and Infidels*, p. 41.
6. RGI, "God in the Constitution," *Works*, vol. 11, pp. 124–125.
7. RGI, "Thomas Paine," *Works*, vol. 1, p. 128.
8. Ibid., p. 134.
9. Ibid., p. 133.
10. Ibid., p. 153.

11. Ibid., p. 164.
12. Moncure Daniel Conway, *The Life of Thomas Paine* (New York, 1892), vol. 2, p. 428.
13. RGI, "Thomas Paine," *North American Review*, August 1892.
14. See Michael Kazin, *A Godly Hero: The Life of William Jennings Bryan* (New York, 2006), pp. 9–11.
15. RGI, "Some Mistakes of Moses," *Works*, vol. 2, p. 31.
16. Ibid., p. 32.
17. RGI, "Our Schools," *Works*, vol. 11, pp. 471–472.

CHAPTER VI
Reason and Passion

1. Susan B. Anthony, *Diary*, April 14, 1854, quoted in Carol Kolmerten, *The American Life of Ernestine Rose* (Syracuse, NY, 1999), p. 155.
2. RGI, "At a Child's Grave," *Works*, vol. 12, p. 400.
3. RGI, "A Lay Sermon," *Works*, vol. 4, p. 211.
4. RGI to George Schilling, in Ingersoll, *Letters*, pp. 627–628.
5. Ibid., p. 216.
6. *The Kreutzer Sonata and Other Stories*, translated by Louise and Aylmer Maude and J. D. Duff (New York, 1997), pp. 110–111.
7. RGI, "Tolstoi and 'The Kreutzer Sonata,'" *Works*, vol. 11, p. 313.
8. RGI, "Which Way?" *Works*, vol. 3, p. 401.
9. Ibid., pp. 448–449.
10. RGI to Philip G. Peabody, May 27, 1890, in *The Letters of Robert G. Ingersoll*, pp. 710–711.
11. "Vivisection," *New York Evening Telegram*, September 30, 1893.
12. RGI to Peabody, May 27, 1890, in Ingersoll, *Letters*, p. 711.

CHAPTER VII
Death and Afterlife

1. RGI, "Argument Before the Vice-Chancellor in the Russell Case," *Works*, vol. 10, p. 592.
2. "Ingersoll Dead," *New York Times*, July 22, 1899.
3. RGI, "A Tribute to Ebon C. Ingersoll," *Works*, vol. 12, p. 390.

4. Ibid., p. 391.
5. In Cramer, *Royal Bob*, p. 264.
6. "Sermons on Ingersoll," *Chicago Tribune*, July 24, 1899.
7. In Cramer, *Royal Bob*, p. 189, from unedited clippings in Library of Congress, folder 5.
8. *Truth Seeker*, October 21, 1899.
9. *The Chicago Tribune*, July 22, 1899.
10. In Frank Smith, *Robert G. Ingersoll: A Life* (Buffalo, NY, 1990), p. 403.
11. In Larson, *American Infidel*, from *Arena*, March 1909.
12. William Bentley, *The Diary of William Bentley* (Salem, MA, 1905), vol. 1, p. 82.
13. In "Ingersoll Still Troubling the World," *Current Literature*, December 1911 (article unsigned).
14. George E. Webb, *The Evolution Controversy in America* (Lexington, KY), 1994, pp. 110–114.
15. Michael Monahan, "In re Colonel Ingersoll," *An Attic Dreamer* (New York, 1922), pp. 62–63.

Selected Bibliography

Anderson, David D. *Robert Ingersoll*. New York: Twayne, 1972.

Allen, Frederick Lewis, *Only Yesterday*. New York: Harper and Brothers, 1931.

Avrich, Paul. *The Haymarket Tragedy*. Princeton, NJ: Princeton University Press, 1984.

Bentley, William. *The Diary of William Bentley*, vols. 1–4. Salem, MA: Essex Institute, 1905.

Borden, Morton. *Jews, Turks, and Infidels*. Chapel Hill: University of North Carolina Press, 1984.

Brigance, Willaim Norwood, ed. *A History and Criticism of American Public Address*. Vols. 1–2. New York: McGraw-Hill, 1943.

Burns, Robert. *The Poetical Works of Robert Burns*. Ed. Raymond Bentman. Boston: Houghton Mifflin, 1974.

Conway, Moncure Daniel. *The Life of Thomas Paine*. Vols. 1–2. New York: Cassell, 1892.

Cramer, C. H. *Royal Bob: The Life of Robert G. Ingersoll*. Indianapolis: Bobbs-Merrill, 1952.

Darrow, Clarence. *The Story of My Life.* New York: Grosset and Dunlap, 1932.

Darrow, Clarence, and Wallace Rice. *Infidels and Heretics.* Boston: Alpine Press, 1929.

Darwin, Charles. *On the Origin of Species: The Orgin of Species by Means of Natural Selection; or, the Preservation of Favoured Races in the Struggle for Life* and *The Descent of Man and Selection in Relation to Sex.* New York: Modern Library, 1948.

Fruchtman, Jack, Jr. *Thomas Paine: Apostle of Freedom.* New York: Four Walls Eight Windows, 1994.

Garland, Hamlin. *Roadside Meetings.* New York: Macmillan, 1930.

Greeley, Roger. E. *Ingersoll: Immortal Infidel.* Buffalo, NY: Prometheus Books, 1977.

Hofstadter, Richard: *Anti-Intellectualism in American Life.* New York: Knopf, 1963.

———. *Social Darwinism in American Thought.* New York: George Braziller, 1959.

Hubbard, Elbert. *Little Journey to the Home of Robert G. Ingersoll.* East Aurora, NY: Roycrofters, 1902.

Ingersoll, Robert Green. *The Complete Works of Robert G. Ingersoll.* vols. 1–12. New York: Dresden, 1901.

———. *Letters.* With a biographical introduction by Eva Ingersoll Wakefield. New York: Philosophical Library, 1951.

Irons, Peter. A People's History of the Supreme Court. New York: Penguin Books, 1999.

Jacoby, Susan. *Freethinkers: A History of American Secularism.* New York: Metropolitan Books, 2004.

Kazin, Michael. *A Godly Hero.* New York: Knopf, 2006.

Kolmerten, Carol A. *The American Life of Ernestine L. Rose.* Syracuse, NY: Syracuse University Press, 1999.

Larson, Orvin. *American Infidel: Robert G. Ingersoll.* New York: Citadel Press, 1962.

Lincoln, Abraham. *Collected Works of Abraham Lincoln*, vols. 5–7. Ed. Roy P. Basler, Marion Dolores Pratt, and Lloyd C. Dunlap. New Brunswick, NJ: Rutgers University Press, 1953–1955.

MacDonald, George E. *Fifty Years of Freethought*, vols. 1–2. New York: Truth Seeker Company, 1959.

Marty, Martin E. *Modern American Religion*, vols. 1–3. Chicago: University of Chicago Press, 1986–1996.

Monahan, Michael. *An Attic Dreamer.* New York: Mitchell Kennerley, 1922.

Mott, James R. *The Post-Darwinian Controversies.* Cambridge: Cambridge University Press, 1979.

Paine, Thomas. *The Thomas Paine Reader.* Ed. Michael Foot and Isaac Kramnick. New York: Penguin Books, 1987.

———. *The Complete Writings of Thomas Paine.* Ed. Philip S. Foner. New York: Citadel Press, 1945.

Peck, Harry Thurston. *What Is Good English? And Other Essays.* New York: Dodd, Mead, 1899.

Plummer, Mark A. *Robert G. Ingersoll: Peoria's Pagan Politician.* Macomb, IL: Western Illinois Monograph Series, 1984.

Ritter, Lawrence S. *The Glory of Their Times: The Story of the Early Days of Baseball Told by the Men Who Played It.* New York: Harper Perennial Modern Classics. 1962.

Rogers, Cameron. *Colonel Bob Ingersoll.* New York: Doubleday, Page, 1927.

Roosevelt, Theodore. *Gouverneur Morris.* Oyster Bay, NY: Theodore Roosevelt Association, 1975.

Tolstoy, Leo. *The Kreutzer Sonata and Other Stories.* Ed. Richard J. Gustafson. Translated by Louise and Aylmer Maude and J. D. Duff. New York: Oxford University Press, 1997.

Truth Seeker. Vols. 10–37. New York: Truth Seeker Company, 1883–1910.

Twain, Mark. *The Bible According to Mark Twain.* Ed. Howard G. Baetzhold and Joseph B. McCullough. New York: Touchstone Books, 1996.

Vowell, Sarah. *Assassination Vacation*. New York: Simon and
Schuster, 2005.
Warren, Sidney. *American Freethought, 1860–1914*. New York:
Columbia University Press, 1943.
Webb, George E. *The Evolution Controversy in America*.
Lexington: University Press of Kentucky, 1994.
Whitman, Walt. *Leaves of Grass*. New York: Modern Library,
1921.

Index

American Centennial (July 4,
1876), 5
American Federation of
Musicians, 160
American founders. *See*
founders
American Free Religious
Association, 171
American politics. *See* politics
and government
*American Religious Identification
Survey*, 30n
American Revolution, Paine's
writings and, 1, 18, 19,
142–43, 146, 147
American Secular Union,
131–32, 162, 163
anesthesia, 78, 79
animal experiments. *See*
vivisection
Anthony, Susan B., 73, 157
anthrax, 80
anti-obscenity laws. *See*
obscenity (Comstock) laws
anti-Semitism, 114
"Apostate's Creed" (anon.), 85
Arlington National Cemetery,
176
Arthur, Chester A., 115
asceticism, 164–66
asepsis, 79
Atchison (Kansas) Daily Globe,
27
atheists. *See* agnostics/atheists;
"new atheists"
atonement, 88
autodidacts, 7–8, 36, 38, 42–43,
44

bacteria, 5, 79, 80
Baptists, 145
Barlow, Joel, 40
Barton, Clara, 10
Baxter, Richard, *The Saint's
Everlasting Rest*, 37
Beckwith, Philo D., 72, 73–74,
190
Beckworth Memorial Theater
(Dowagiac, MI), 72–76, 190
Beecher, Rev. Henry Ward, 16,
54, 90, 91–94, 96; Ingersoll
eulogy for, 92–93; social
beliefs of, 108
Beecher, Rev. Lyman, 92, 93
Beethoven, Ludwig van, 73,
161, 190
Bennett, William D., 99
Bentley, Rev. William, 181
Bible, 13, 21, 38–39, 44, 96,
175; creation account of, 9,
14, 16, 80–82, 86–88, 104,
149; liberal Protestant view
of, 182; as literal (*see* biblical
literalism); as literary/
philosophical work, 153; as
metaphoric, 148; officeholders' sworn oath on, 136–37;
as sanctioning corporal
punishment, 39; as sanctioning death penalty, 144, 199;
as sanctioning slavery, 52–53,
140; as sanctioning women's
inferiority, 122
Bible Institute of Los Angeles,
The Fundamentals, 101n
biblical literalism, 11, 14;
blasphemy law and, 131–36,

Catholicism (*continued*)
152; political influence of,
66–67, 100–101, 121, 139,
141, 185; Protestant domi-
nance and, 65, 66, 177;
religious school system of,
64–66, 100–101, 141, 153,
154, 183, 185; suspicion of
science and, 141, 183; U.S.
presidential candidacy and,
4n
Catholic World (publication), 184
Cazenovia (NY), 35
chastity, 164, 165
Chicago, 73, 162, 177–78
Chicago Times, 59
Chicago Tribune, 174, 177, 180
childbearing: pain alleviation
and, 78; women's rights and,
118–19, 127, 152. *See also*
birth control
children's rights, 39–40, 200
Chinese Exclusion Act (1882),
114–15
Chinese immigrants, 114–16
Chopin, Frédéric, 73
Christianity: founders and, 4, 9,
98–99, 129, 137–39, 200;
Ingersoll's stance on, 58, 114,
164–66; political officeholders and, 54–55, 137, 178–79;
proposed constitutional
amendment endorsing,
98–99, 139; secular constitution and, 195; status of
women and, 122–23, 164–65.
See also Catholicism;
Protestantism

Church of England, 13
church-state separation, 129–55;
blasphemy law and, 135;
Catholic doctrinal campaign
against, 185–86; Christian
nation contention vs., 4, 9,
98–99, 129, 139; continuing
lack of public consensus on,
9; current political decriers
of, 4, 136, 201; divine authority invocation and,
150–51; divorce laws and,
120–21; establishment clause
and, 64–65, 136; first Catholic
presidential candidate and,
4n; as founders' intent, 2–5,
129, 137, 138, 139–40, 141,
150, 195, 197, 200–201;
Ingersoll's championship of,
1–5, 11, 20–21, 139–42,
150–51; Jewish immigrant
support for, 70; Lincoln
Republicans and, 61, 99;
obscenity (Comstock) laws
and, 100; opponents of,
135–38, 185–86; Paine's
championship of, 1, 18, 20,
107; public schools and, 9,
105, 142, 153–55, 186–87;
religious orthodoxy vs., 69,
152–53; religious politiciza-
tion and, 151–52; religious
school tax aid bid and, 4n,
64–66, 67, 70, 100–101, 153,
154, 183, 185; secularist
inroads and, 148; state law
changes and, 138; theocracy
vs., 58, 98, 129, 136, 200, 201

communication of complex subjects by, 88–90, 187, 195, 198–99; as corporal punishment opponent, 39–40; critical causes of, 39, 109; cultural interests of, 160–61; current obscurity of, 9, 19–20, 22, 26–27, 193–202; current relevance of, 201–2; Darrow's view of, 102–3; death concept of, 157–58; death of, 7, 20–21, 22, 173–80; Debs eulogy for, 179–80; diverse audience for, 11–12, 182, 187; domestic happiness of, 21–22, 117, 123, 173–74; economic views of, 10, 103–7; Edison sound recording of, 97; eulogy for Beecher of, 92–93; eulogy for brother of, 175–76; eulogy for Whitman of, 75, 206–11; fame of, 1, 42, 68; finances of, 20, 174, 180; funeral and grave of, 175–76; generosity of, 174; "gospel of humanity" of, 159–63; as Great Agnostic, 1, 9, 12, 37, 68, 153, 156, 179, 193; "happiness creed" of, 97, 162, 175, 189; Haymarket defendants and, 162–63; illness/last weeks of, 171, 172–73; influence of, 7, 10, 92, 95, 159, 182; last two public appearances of, 171–72; lecture audiences for, 2–3, 7, 8, 11–15, 21, 25, 57–58, 68–73, 94, 131–32, 187; legacies of, 1, 9–10, 193–202;

legal career of, 7, 11, 21, 48, 49, 53, 58, 68, 69, 101–2, 131–36, 142–43, 171–72; literary favorites of, 42–48, 94, 123, 153, 156, 161, 174–75; on meaning of life, 157; as national figure, 59–60; "new atheists" and, 17, 193–202; optimism of, 84–85, 127, 167–69; oratorical gifts of, 8–9, 12–15, 19, 23, 42, 45, 53, 59–61, 68, 75–86, 88–90, 95–96; Paine's influence on, 1, 18, 143–48, 189, 193; physical size of, 8; political office bids of, 50, 54–55, 57; political ties of, 10, 11, 27, 50–55, 57–61, 63–71, 97–98, 100, 101–3, 163, 178–79, 200–201; political views of, 97–98; popular lectures of, 40–41, 71; posthumous reactions to, 181–86, 189–91, 196; press obituaries/editorials on, 22, 27, 173–75, 178–81; publicizing methods of, 45; religious critics' characterization of, 156–57; romantic chivalry of, 123; scientific/technological progress belief of, 78, 79–80, 95–96; secular government cause of, 1–5, 11, 20–21, 139–42, 150–51; secularism definition of, 125–27; secularist creed of, 161–62; as self-made American archetype, 7–8, 36, 38, 42–43;